T0316666

Cambridge Elements

Elements in the Philosophy of Religion
edited by
Yujin Nagasawa
University of Birmingham

RELIGIOUS DIVERSITY AND RELIGIOUS PROGRESS

Robert McKim
University of Illinois, Urbana-Champaign

CAMBRIDGE
UNIVERSITY PRESS

CAMBRIDGE
UNIVERSITY PRESS

University Printing House, Cambridge CB2 8BS, United Kingdom

One Liberty Plaza, 20th Floor, New York, NY 10006, USA

477 Williamstown Road, Port Melbourne, VIC 3207, Australia

314–321, 3rd Floor, Plot 3, Splendor Forum, Jasola District Centre,
New Delhi – 110025, India

79 Anson Road, #06–04/06, Singapore 079906

Cambridge University Press is part of the University of Cambridge.

It furthers the University's mission by disseminating knowledge in the pursuit of
education, learning, and research at the highest international levels of excellence.

www.cambridge.org
Information on this title: www.cambridge.org/9781108457552
DOI: 10.1017/9781108558419

First published 2019

A catalogue record for this publication is available from the British Library.

ISBN 978-1-108-45755-2 Paperback
ISSN 2399-5165 (online)
ISSN 2515-9763 (print)

Religious Diversity and Religious Progress

Elements in Philosophy of Religion

DOI: 10.1017/9781108558419
First published online: January 2019

Robert McKim
University of Illinois, Urbana-Champaign

Abstract: What is someone who has a perspective on religious matters to say about those who endorse other perspectives? What should he or she say about other religions? For example, might some of their beliefs be true? What stage are we human beings at in our religious development? Are we close to maturity, religiously speaking, so that most of the important religious ideas and innovations there will ever be have already appeared? Or are we starting out in our religious evolution, so that religious developments to date are merely the first rude efforts of a species in its religious infancy?

Keywords: religious diversity, religious pluralism, religious progress

ISBNs: 9781108457552 (PB), 9781108558419 (OC)
ISSNs: 2399-5165 (online), 2515-9763 (print)

Contents

1 Religious Others

1.1 Introduction

What is someone who has a perspective on religious matters to say about those who endorse other perspectives? For example, what is an insider to a religious tradition, a member of the "home tradition," to say about outsiders, which is to say those who neither endorse the insider's religious perspective nor engage in the insider's religious practice?

Insiders – members of the home tradition – sometimes take the view that there is something seriously wrong with outsiders. Thus some insiders contend that the failure of outsiders to endorse their favored beliefs, the endorsement by outsiders of competing beliefs, and, in general, the failure of outsiders to live the life associated with the insiders' religion have their origin in sinfulness or wickedness or perversity or rebelliousness or arrogance or laziness or a failure to think things through, or in being too preoccupied with the passing scene or in some other such defect or set of defects. Outsiders may even be seen as childish or laughable or ridiculous or contemptible or deserving of pity.

On the other hand, insiders sometimes take the very different view that outsiders are, or can be, about as impressive as insiders, all things considered. For example, in their essay "Thinking Outside the Box: Developments in Catholic Understandings of Salvation," Daniel A. Madigan and Diego R. Sarrió Cucarella deploy the idea of *orientation* in the course of explaining what they consider to be the correct perspective for Catholics to have on non-Catholics. These authors say that "[what] has gradually come to be realized over the centuries is that, although many good people are not explicitly members of the Church, they are in effect oriented in the same way. As the Church is oriented to the Reign of God, and hence to Christ, we recognize others who are in effect facing, striving even, in the same direction – desiring the same justice, love and peace that are to be the hallmarks of the Reign of God" (Madigan and Sarrió, 2016: 101).

Moreover, the view of these authors is that God is on the side of a correctly oriented person with no affiliation with the institutional Church to a greater extent than God is on the side of an incorrectly oriented member of the Church. They write that "[there] will be insiders who will not be well oriented to the Reign of God – we all have to admit that at times we ourselves are among them – and there will be outsiders who are admirably oriented to that Reign" and that "it is now recognized that neither actual membership in the Church, nor even an explicit desire for membership, is essential in order for God to orient a person or community toward life in Him" (Madigan and Sarrió, 2016: 103, 110). In general, these authors say that outsiders may be as impressive as insiders in various important respects. However, as hinted in the sentence I just quoted, their view is also that the correct explanation of cases in which outsiders are correctly oriented is uniquely Christian.

And might outsiders be reasoning just as carefully, and be just as reasonable in their beliefs, as insiders? For example, in his essay "The Islamic Problem of Religious Diversity," Imran Aijaz contends that there is very strong, indeed, in his view, "overwhelming," empirical evidence for the claim that some rational and inculpable nonacceptance of Islamic belief occurs; this is just to say that the claim that there is no rational and inculpable nonacceptance of Islamic belief – a claim he characterizes as traditionally Islamic – is mistaken (Aijaz, 2016: 167). In this essay Imran Aijaz also considers, and rejects, various attempts to deny that there is rational and inculpable nonacceptance of Islamic belief. These include attempts to argue that those who appear not to endorse Islamic belief *only appear* not to do so – that such people secretly and "in their hearts" actually hold Islamic belief to be true. Other attempts to deny that there is rational and inculpable nonacceptance of Islamic belief contend that disobedience and sin are the root cause of nonacceptance of Islamic beliefs so that this nonacceptance is culpable.

These conclusions, incidentally, lead Imran Aijaz to argue that two additional claims – both of which he also characterizes as traditional Islamic ones – are also mistaken. These are the claims that (a) very strong epistemic justification for Islamic belief is available to everyone, which is just to say that everyone has good reason to recognize the truth of Islamic beliefs, and that (b) little or no epistemic justification is available to anyone for holding beliefs incompatible with Islamic belief. And he proposes that Muslim thinkers may therefore wish to rethink their views about non-Muslims and may, in particular, wish to revise radically their concept of a *kafir* (disbeliever).

1.2 Religion That Says That Outsiders Have Something Seriously Wrong with Them and That This Accounts for Their Being Outsiders

To be sure, whatever may be our religious perspective, it is difficult to avoid the thought that religious others are below par with us in one particular respect. Anyone who does not endorse our perspective will normally be thought by us to be mistaken and to be missing something important, assuming that the question of what to say about them and their views arises, and an opinion about these matters is formed. If we are to be consistent, we are committed to the belief that those who disagree with us are mistaken so that, at least in this particular respect, they have a deficiency or flaw that we do not have. If we are right, they are wrong.

What is problematic and unfortunate, however, is the idea that what insiders consider to be the mistaken religious views of outsiders, or the fact that outsiders do not endorse (and may reject) the views of insiders, is best accounted for by, say, human foolishness or sinfulness or wickedness or perversity. There are two problematic ideas here. First, there is the idea that religious outsiders suffer from such serious defects as these. And, second, there is the idea that this accounts for their holding their views or, more broadly, for their being the way they are, religiously speaking.

In another paper, Imran Aijaz mentions some cases in which nonbelief is traced to various putative serious flaws, citing Muslim and Christian examples. In the Muslim case, he quotes from Wilfred Cantwell Smith, who wrote in the course of explaining what Islam has to say about these matters that "Kufr (so-called 'infidelity'), the heinous sin, the incomprehensibly stupid and perverse obduracy, is not unbelief but 'refusal.' It is almost a spitting in God's face when He speaks out of His infinite authority and vast compassion. It is man's dramatic negative response to this spectacular divine initiative" (Aijaz, 2013: 406). And Imran Aijaz quotes from Toshihiko Izutsu, who writes that "the Koranic system reveals a very simple structure based on a clearcut distinction between Muslims and Kâfirs. All Muslims are members of the community . . . And they stand in sharp opposition to those who . . . refuse to listen seriously to Muhammad's teaching and to believe in God" (Aijaz, 2013: 406).

Imran Aijaz mentions too the contention of Christian philosopher William Lane Craig that "when a person refuses to come to Christ, it is never just because of lack of evidence or because of intellectual difficulties: at root, he refuses to come because he willingly ignores and rejects the drawing of God's Spirit on his heart. No one in the final analysis really fails to become a Christian because of lack of arguments; he fails to become a Christian because he loves darkness rather than light and wants nothing to do with God" (Aijaz, 2013: 413). And he also cites the claim of Alvin Plantinga that "[w]ere it not for sin and its effects, God's presence and glory would be as obvious and uncontroversial to us all as the presence of other minds, physical objects, and the past" (Aijaz, 2013: 414).

Now proposals in this area differ in significant ways; indeed, this is so even for the few examples I just provided. Such proposals vary with respect to the extent to which they take nonbelief to be culpable, which is just to say something for which people may reasonably be blamed. For example, nonbelief that issues from original sin or from, say, an inability to understand a complex piece of reasoning may not be the sort of thing for which it is appropriate to blame someone. On the other hand, wickedness, perversity, willingly ignoring what one would otherwise be aware of, and loving darkness rather than light have the air of culpability about them. However, even in the case in which a failure to believe may seem relatively innocent given the condition or state someone is in, they may be blameworthy for being in that condition or state. Thus a person who does not hold a belief because a complex piece of reasoning that suffices to establish it, and to which he or she she has been exposed, is beyond his or her grasp might be blameworthy for not having cultivated sufficiently her ability to reason. And people might be *partly* to blame, either for failing to believe or for any deficiencies that cause them to do so.

So there are at any rate some strands in these major religious traditions according to which outsiders are seriously flawed, and according to which the relevant flaws are understood to account for their being outsiders. Unfortunately, many people seem to find it easy to go along with the denigration of others that this involves. Whether or not they say this out loud, their attitude to others is along these lines: "Not only is it the case that we are right and you are wrong, what explains this situation is that you, unlike us, are wicked or sinful."

There is often a great deal at stake. For how we think of others can matter profoundly. A situation in which some others are viewed negatively in such fundamental respects as these is risky. Chances are that the relevant others will understand how they are being perceived. They may resent it and if they have a chance they may retaliate. Tensions may arise and the idea that others are wicked or perverse or the like may exacerbate those tensions. Concern about the relevant others – about, say, their welfare or their troubles or the traumas they experience or whether they achieve their aspirations – may be diminished and *this* can have harmful consequences. Worse still, viewing others negatively may make it easier to acquiesce in, say, their being killed or injured or displaced in an unjust war perpetrated by one's coreligionists. The thought might even be that since outsiders are going to hell anyway, there is no great harm in giving them a nudge along the way. Or since God will eventually punish them, there is no great harm in our getting the process of punishment started here and now.

Yasir Qadhi, a Muslim scholar, probes the practical implications of one very negative view of outsiders. He quotes these remarks from Rousseau's *The Social Contract*: "It is impossible to live in peace with those one believes to be damned. To love them would be to hate God who punishes them. It is absolutely necessary either to reclaim them or to torment them" (Qadhi, 2013: 109).[1] And he asks,

---

[1] This contention from Rousseau certainly is absurd. What accounts for it? It is part of an exuberant sales pitch Rousseau makes in book 4, chapter 8 of *The Social Contract* for what he calls "civil religion." Civil religion consists in a few sentiments that, in his view, are essential to being a good

"[how] can one treat another person with dignity knowing full well that God has damned him or her?" (Qadhi, 2013: 118).

Qadhi's own approach to this matter has two parts. He makes the observation that "mainstream Muslims, Sunnis and Shi'is . . . have often managed to live cordially with people of all faiths throughout history and across geographic regions" (Qadhi, 2013: 118). While his point is clearly correct, the more relevant question is whether Muslims *who believe that God has damned the others in question* have generally managed to live cordially with them. And I think his view is that the correct answer to this question is "yes," which is in effect to say that he rejects Rousseau's absurd claim to the contrary.

Second, Yasir more or less rules out the possibility that anyone could know in the case of a particular person that God has damned them. While he endorses the exclusivist view that rejection of Islam makes one ineligible for salvation, he says that this is so only if one rejects Islam *after one has been exposed to Islam properly.* "God's punishment awaits only those who have received and understood the prophetic message and then willingly and knowingly rejected it" (Qadhi, 2013: 119). Since God alone can judge whether any particular person has been properly exposed to Islam – which he takes to be a matter of having received and understood the prophetic message – it is impossible for anyone to know which individuals are ineligible for salvation. The upshot is that since Muslims are not in a position to assess whether a particular non-Muslim has been exposed to Islam properly, and hence whether the fact that that person is a non-Muslim will result in her being damned, the issue of how to treat people whom one believes to have been damned should not arise in practice. Still, as Yasir acknowledges, the idea that outsiders who have been properly exposed to Islam are damned – even if we add the qualification that we do not know who is in this category – can encourage prejudice and intolerance.

These remarks from Yasir Qadhi raise the question of how the idea of being exposed to Islam *properly* is best understood. Obviously much the same question arises in the case of other religions that consider a person's beliefs to have a bearing on their salvific status, and especially when proper exposure

---

citizen. These include belief in a God, an afterlife, the reward of the just, the punishment of evildoers, the sanctity of the social contract between the sovereign and the citizens, and, crucially, tolerance of all religions that tolerate others. He endeavors to show the appeal of civil religion by casting various religious alternatives in a negative light – in particular, as involving beliefs about others that will foster social strife. Naturally one wonders why civil religion cannot tolerate groups that *tolerate* those they believe to be damned. For, contrary to what Rousseau says, this occurs. More to the point, a toned-down and more modest claim along these lines is not absurd at all: belief that others around us are damned can have very harmful consequences.

to those beliefs followed by rejection of them is understood to render one ineligible for salvation. I consider this issue of proper exposure in more detail in Section 3.

In his book *States of Ireland*, Conor Cruise O'Brien comments on related themes, this time with a focus on the Northern Ireland conflict: "In theory Irish Catholics and Ulster Protestants shared a religion of love … You were supposed to love your neighbour, even of the 'opposite' religion, but as his beliefs and behaviour were obviously so offensive as to mark him out for hell-fire it didn't seem to matter if you knocked him about a bit in this life, if only to prepare him for what was coming to him in the next" (O'Brien, 1972: 308).

However, it goes without saying that there is no reason to impute the harmful attitudes to others under discussion to the majority of Christians or Muslims even though we have seen a couple of Christian and Muslim examples and it would not be hard to find more, or for that matter to find similar attitudes in other religions. And we should acknowledge that for a host of reasons these matters are very complicated in real life. For one thing, when we deal with religious others, our awareness of them *as* religious others will often be just one of a vast set of interconnected ways in which we think of them. We may think of such a person as, say, a relative, neighbor, coworker, friend, fellow gardener, business partner, employer, fellow supporter of all manner of important causes, someone whom we trust as an expert in this or that area, and so on. The awareness of such a person *as* a religious other may be a relatively minor ingredient in the mix and may be obscured or ignored entirely.

Moreover, even if outsiders *are* thought to have serious flaws, insiders may feel that they have abundant reasons to be on good terms with, and friendly toward, them. For example, insiders may feel that there is much that is good and admirable about outsiders in spite of those putative flaws. Or they may take a "live and let live" attitude or exhibit a generosity that has a softening influence. Or they may feel that sincerely bestowed generosity or kindness to the outsider shows their own faith in the best possible light. They may feel or do these things because their own religious perspective calls on them to do so – which is just to say that their own tradition has its own internal resources for combatting the harmful attitudes in question – or for independent reasons. And even when such attitudes *are* harmful, there may be no way to measure *the extent* to which they are harmful – no way to measure the extent to which they exacerbate tensions, diminish concern that insiders would otherwise have for outsiders, promote hostility, and so on. To complicate matters further, when interreligious tensions make their presence felt, there normally are other differences present too; thus there may be competing political or territorial aspirations or competing historical narratives so that the harmful consequences of religious differences as such may be difficult to discern.

So we should not exaggerate the problem and we should be mindful of complexities such as these. On the other hand, there is no denying the potentially harmful consequences of seeing others as grossly defective – in thinking of them as not just mistaken but as wicked or perverse or the like. After all, whatever defects we attribute to them by way of an explanation of how it is that they disagree with us may have a bearing on, say, *whether* we trust them in other areas or *whether* we befriend them, and so on. And, as I say, tensions *may* arise, and the belief that there is something deeply wrong with them *may* exacerbate those tensions. It happens frequently. There is no escaping the fact that such attitudes can be dangerous. They are also unkind and unimpressive. And we can do much better.

1.3 Religious Ambiguity

The best response to religion that says that outsiders have something seriously wrong with them and that this accounts for their holding their views has a number of components, and I lay these out in the remainder of Section 1.

For one thing, we have available a better explanation of why others disagree with us about religious matters.

This better explanation is that the human situation is religiously ambiguous. What I mean by this, in brief, is that the following conditions hold. (I pursue this topic in more detail in McKim, 2012: chapter 7, and I draw on that discussion here.) There is a significant amount of evidence for more than one religious perspective; none of the competing perspectives can be proven correct and the evidence does not clearly favor one perspective over the others; each group has its own evidence to which it can appeal; the evidence as a whole is diverse in its character, multifaceted, and complicated; and the evidence is so abundant that a comprehensive perspective that is developed by taking account of all of it is out of the question. Only a partial perspective is feasible, and the task of disambiguating the situation currently far exceeds our abilities.

If the human religious situation is ambiguous, matters of religious significance are open to being reasonably interpreted in a variety of ways, and no position on religious matters that is currently endorsed is obviously correct. Consensus about matters of religious significance is unlikely to occur, and the pursuit of truth in this area, even when engaged in with effort, care, and sincerity – and whether engaged in individually or at the communal level, and however skilled those who engage in it may be – is unlikely to lead everyone to the same conclusions. The situation would be entirely different if, say, atheism or Sunni Islam or Roman Catholicism or some type of animism were clearly correct in its claims about how things are. But it is not so.

Many religious people consider religious experiences they enjoy to be part of their evidence for their religious perspective. (Or at any rate, if questioned and if they had an opportunity to reflect on the matter, they would agree that this is so.) For example, many people who believe that there is a God understand, say, a sense that God is guiding them or strengthening them or inspiring them to be part of their evidence that there is a God. Some people who understand their own religious experiences to be part of their relevant evidence are willing to take another step and to consider the religious experiences of others to be part of the total evidence that pertains to what is true in the area of religion.[2] If they are correct, and I think they are, then for this reason alone no one can have access to all of the available evidence. In particular, each of us lacks access to what it would be like to endorse, and live in accordance with, numerous other perspectives, with whatever experiences are attendant upon doing so.

1.4 Religious Ambiguity and Religious Others

Because of religious ambiguity, the fact that there are outsiders who do not believe what we believe is not such a great puzzle and it is unnecessary and unreasonable to suppose that there is anything seriously wrong with others in virtue of their not believing as we believe. Ambiguity provides a way to liberate people from such thoughts. Shortly I argue that it provides part of the foundation for a broader approach to others that avoids attributing serious flaws to them.

In general religious ambiguity provides a positive and pleasing way to explain religious diversity. It provides a way to combine the idea that we – whoever we may be – are right with the idea that others are about as reasonable as we are even if, in our view, they are wrong. It enables us to see it as understandable that outsiders disagree with us and that they are not that impressed by what we have to say and not that attracted by what we have to offer. And this includes outsiders who have heard what we have to say but who are not convinced, and who have therefore ignored or failed to respond to, or who may even have rejected, what we consider most valuable. For what a recognition of ambiguity commits us to is that positions other than our own have associated with them bodies of evidence to which their adherents can appeal and that positions other than our own can therefore be rationally endorsed.

---

[2] This move is central to John Hick's defense of his pluralistic hypothesis. See, e.g., Hick (1989: 228).

Even if we know little about what makes the views of others reasonable, such as the character of their distinctive religious experiences, we should at least be aware that there probably is much that does so. And if we don't know what it is, we might set out to try to learn something about it. And we might consider that for us not to know about it probably is as much a matter of a flaw in us as it is a matter of a flaw in them, and it may well be neither. Moreover, once we acknowledge the fact of religious ambiguity we can readily see through attempts to discredit those who disagree with us religiously by attributing serious flaws to them.

Religious ambiguity can even help us to understand those particular "outsiders" who used to be insiders: that is, those who used to endorse what we believe but who have changed their minds and no longer do so, perhaps even rejecting their former beliefs. Given ambiguity, it is not surprising that people sometimes change their minds. And this is so for two reasons, at least: first, their antecedently held position is not clearly correct and, second, there are other perspectives that have a lot going for them, and this may apply to their newly adopted perspective. It may have its own body of sustaining evidence.

I say "*may* have its own body of sustaining evidence" for there is no reason to think that everyone who endorses other positions does so rationally, or even that *most* people who endorse other positions do so rationally. Surely there must be cases in which flaws may legitimately be imputed to those who disagree with us and, more to the point, in which their not believing as we believe may legitimately be traced to those flaws. The implausible idea that all failure to believe as we believe arises from, say, perversity or wickedness is completely different from the plausible idea that there are *cases* of unbelief that arise from some such serious defect. It would be unwise to propose that *all* religious diversity is to be accounted for by appeal to religious ambiguity.

Correspondingly, though, we should not assume that everyone who endorses *our* position, whatever it may be, does so rationally. Probably a good operating assumption is that whatever flaws are relevant in the case of others are as likely to be found within our group as they are to be found in theirs. Wickedness, perversity, carelessness, laziness, conformism, failing to ask important questions when you ought to do so, and the like are as likely to account for *our* holding or retaining our beliefs as they are to account for others doing so. Indeed, such flaws probably are about as widely distributed among us as they are among others – especially if we extend our purview across countries, cultures, and historical epochs. Roughly speaking, we are all doing equally well in terms of belief management. These are, at any rate, good operating assumptions – positions to be endorsed until given reason to believe otherwise.

1.5 Recognizing Our Own Deficiencies and Recognizing That Others May Be Suffering from No More Deficiencies Than One's Coreligionists

There is a certain sort of awareness of being deficient – that is, of their own deficiencies – that *all* people with a perspective on religious matters should share. This arises in part from the fact that a vast array of relevant considerations bear on the plausibility of the claims of religious traditions. The vast amount of relevant religious experience is one subset of these relevant considerations, but only one among many.

So a sincere and observant Muslim, for example, might acknowledge that he she lacks an understanding of, say, the Wesleyan idea of sanctification or of the experiences reported on by those who believe themselves to be in this state of sanctification or of what it is like to live in earnest expectation of achieving it, assuming that he or she indeed lacks this understanding. Or a devoted Catholic might acknowledge that he or she has no understanding of the Buddhist idea of a Bodhisattva, or of what it is like to live in the grip of this idea of postponing your own final release and serving as a "refuge" or "shelter" until everyone has achieved enlightenment, and to see yourself as playing this self-sacrificial role in the lives of others, assuming that he or she lacks this understanding. Or a devout Lutheran might admit that he or she has no understanding of Navajo religion, of its implications for how we should treat nonhuman animals, or of what it is like to experience the world around us, including nonhuman animals, while looking at things in this way. And so on. And this is just to mention some relevant *religious experiences*. The vast array of relevant considerations that bear on the plausibility of the claims of the religious traditions also includes, for example, developments in cosmology and in neuroscience that bear on the plausibility or the meaning of various religious claims. There is abundant scope here for everyone to acknowledge his or her limitations – limitations that in this case are entirely unavoidable and hence inculpable. To do so is far better than to find fault with outsiders.

Moreover, many perspectives on religious matters are endorsed by people of integrity. By "people of integrity" I mean people who, at least in the ideal case, know a great deal, avoid exaggeration, admit ignorance when appropriate, have an interest in the truth, and are sincere, decent, reflective, and so on. People of this caliber can be found in many religious traditions, and, indeed, among those who endorse secular perspectives.[3] I propose both that such people are no more common in any one tradition than they are in the others and that people who approximate to this ideal to one degree or another are similarly distributed.

---

[3] I discuss this topic further and probe some of its implications in McKim (2001: 129ff.).

At any rate, these too are reasonable operating assumptions, default positions to be endorsed until given a compelling reason to believe otherwise. The same goes for the assumption that outsiders are reasoning just as carefully, and are as reasonable in their beliefs as insiders. This too should be endorsed until we have a compelling reason to believe otherwise.

1.6 Another Reason It Is Unlikely That the Deficiencies of Others Account for Their Religious Perspective

To make these judgments about the human religious situation – for example, that the human religious situation is ambiguous and that others may well be neither more nor less deficient than we are, all things considered – will be sobering for many people. For example, atheists may find it difficult and a challenge to adopt views such as these about theists, and vice versa.

However, if you find unconvincing these responses to the contentions that outsiders have something seriously wrong with them and that this accounts for their holding their views, you might find persuasive the following simple observation. In general, people acquire their religious beliefs from their family and community and the culture in which they were raised. John Hick puts it well, though I assume he intended the figure of "ninety-nine per cent" in these remarks to be a loose approximation:

> [In] some ninety-nine per cent of cases the religion which an individual professes and to which he or she adheres depends upon the accidents of birth. Someone born to Buddhist parents in Thailand is very likely to be a Buddhist, someone born to Muslim parents in Saudi Arabia to be a Muslim, someone born to Christian parents in Mexico to be a Christian, and so on. (Hick, 1989: 2)

Just because people acquire their religious beliefs from their family and community and culture, it is unlikely that their being flawed or deficient in any respect accounts for their believing as they do. Indeed, a recognition that we – whoever we may be – are as we are religiously speaking because of the vagaries of parentage, culture, location, historical era, educational opportunities, and the like should lead us to be cautious in attributing to others flaws that allegedly account for their views. Perhaps what really needs to be said is that people who believe what they have been told about complex and controversial matters by, say, their family or their community or their culture, and who do not consider alternatives even though they are well equipped to do so, are failing to take a step they could take and that it would be worthwhile to take; and this may apply to us as readily as it applies to others.

1.7 A More Appropriate Attitude to Religious Others

So how *should* we look on religious others? I advocate what I call the "magna-nimous outlook." This has a number of interconnected components, to some of which I have already alluded. I briefly sketch twelve such components.[4] Indeed, taken together, they can be thought of as a "twelve-step program" for liberating people from the denigration of religious others.

First, this outlook involves seeing both ourselves and others as holding our views under religiously ambiguous circumstances. In this regard we are all fellow travelers on the same road.

Second, there is no need to think that there is anything seriously wrong with others in virtue of their not believing as we believe. We can combine the idea that we are right with the idea that others are about as reasonable as we are even if, in our view, they are wrong. So this outlook rejects any attempt to insult, belittle, stigmatize, or demean religious outsiders, whether explicitly or implicitly.

Third, wickedness, perversity, carelessness, laziness, conformism, failing to ask important questions when you ought to do so, and other such flaws are about as likely to account for members of our group holding or retaining our beliefs as they are to account for others doing so. Such flaws probably are about as widely distributed within our own group as they are within other groups.

Fourth, many perspectives on religious matters are endorsed by people of integrity.

Fifth, others may be reasoning as carefully as we are reasoning. We should not assume that our perspective is so obvious that it recommends itself to everyone. Neither should we assume that our perspective recommends itself to anyone who approaches it in a fair-minded way or with the right set of attitudes – say, humility and an open mind.

Sixth, we should take an exploratory and courteous approach to others and to their views.

Seventh, a certain sort of curiosity about others is appropriate. Curiosity of the relevant sort involves wanting to know about, and being interested in, such others – in, say, their history, ideas, customs, relevant experiences, sacred texts, music, architecture, or languages. It also involves wanting to know what it is like to be them and to have faced the challenges they have faced, wanting to know what has brought them to where they are today, and wanting to know how things look from their point of view.[5] The curiosity that is part of the

---

[4] In this discussion I draw on McKim (2016).

[5] Pamela Sue Anderson writes about the benefits of "learning to see from the point of view of the excluded." In remarks that are suggestive of the importance of ridding ourselves of the idea that

magnanimous outlook also involves a willingness to learn *from* others. It involves openness to the possibility that they may know or reasonably believe something we are unaware of so that we might be able to enrich our perspective by learning from them.

Eighth, this outlook involves appreciating and being happy with religious others more or less as they are and, broadly speaking, being pleased by the idea that they will survive and flourish as they are, if they so wish, and by the thought that their distinct cultural forms will flourish and that they will retain their group identity – assuming, again, that this is their wish. It also involves an absence of any feeling that individuals who disagree with us must come to agree with us, or must join our ranks, in order to be acceptable or to be living well or to flourish in life or the like. Instead we take a relaxed approach to them and to their presence.

Ninth, this outlook involves wishing to maintain, or if necessary to restore or even to create, space that religious others can occupy. Certainly this includes *cultural* space, but it also includes physical space as this too can be in short supply.

Tenth, others cannot reasonably be expected to see things from our point of view, just as we cannot reasonably be expected to see things from theirs. They will inevitably lack access to much that makes our point of view viable, assuming it is indeed viable, just as we will inevitably lack access to much that makes their point of view viable, assuming it is viable.

Eleventh – and here I draw on the emphasis of Madigan and Sarrió on orientation – outsiders may be as successful as insiders at becoming the sort of human being that each of us should become.

Twelfth, this outlook involves openness to collaborative pursuit of religious progress in cooperation with others. We see them as capable of joining us in this pursuit. I say more about this in Section 4.

Central to the liberation that this twelve-step program would facilitate is the thought that not only is there abundant reason to reject the idea that wickedness or perversity or the like accounts for others failing to endorse our views; in addition, the better explanation of why others disagree with us, whatever may be our religious views, involves a recognition that our beliefs are questionable; they may be, and are, reasonably questioned.

---

outsiders have something seriously wrong with them, she writes of "a strange sort of epistemic blindness [that] allows a serious variability in the moral status of humans who differ according to faith, or lack of faith" (Anderson, 2011: 410). The remedy for this ailment, she reasonably proposes, is to see things from outsiders' point of view.

1.8 A Few Clarificatory Remarks

The magnanimous outlook does not involve assuming that the relevant others are free of flaws. Being happy with others more or less as they are, being open to learning from them, being pleased by the idea that they will survive and flourish, judging that many of them are people of integrity or even judging that it is reasonable to assume this, and that the world is richer in virtue of their presence, combined with the various other components of the magnanimous outlook, add up to a rather positive attitude toward them. But none of this requires the thought that others are in no need of improvement just as we may be in need of improvement.

We might say a great deal more about this outlook. For example, we might ponder some reasons why it is appropriate; we might consider its benefits; and we might respond to objections to it. I settle for a few remarks in each of these areas.

Why is the magnanimous outlook appropriate? One line of thought starts with religious ambiguity. For example, the appeal to ambiguity buttresses the case for openness to learning from others, which is a component of magnanimity. In part the appeal here is to the plethora of considerations that sustain the point of view of others. This includes whatever distinctive religious experiences others may enjoy.

As for the *benefits* of this outlook, I will just say that religion that exhibits magnanimity toward others will not be divisive; rather than exacerbating intergroup tensions, it will help to dissipate them. This is because it provides an attractive alternative to the idea that outsiders have something seriously wrong with them that accounts for their being outsiders. Incidentally I am not proposing that the magnanimous outlook provides the only solution to the problem of religion that says that outsiders have serious flaws that account for their being outsiders. That would be implausible. Some religions have internal resources that can help members to combat such attitudes to outsiders. And those who endorse the harmful attitudes in question may have coreligionists who reject those attitudes and who have just as much right to ownership of the tradition and to defining what it stands for. Still, the magnanimous outlook provides a viable response to harmful attitudes to outsiders. It is also attractive for many reasons. It is generous and admirable and, I argue in Section 4, it may help us to prepare for future religious progress.

1.9 An Unconvincing Objection

Finally, I consider an *objection*. Needless to say, many will reject this idea of magnanimity. Some will think it to be unrealistic or to demand too much from people. For example, the proponents of "terror management theory," a social-psychological approach that probes ways in which various ideas about others can promote conflict, probably would consider it unrealistic. Thus the authors of a recently published account of this theory write as follows:

> Because people are aware that there are many different ways of construing reality, confidence in one's worldview and the protection from anxiety that it provides depend on consensual validation from others ... Unfortunately, the mere existence of others with divergent worldviews undermines this consensus, threatens faith in the absolute validity of one's worldview, and reduces its anxiety-buffering effectiveness. People defend against threats posed by alternative worldviews by disparaging them and those who subscribe to them, attempting to convert their adherents to their own worldview, or simply killing them. (Mogahed et al., 2011: 267)

The idea is that religious faith "provides a sense of security, safety, meaning, and comfort in a threatening world" (Mogahed et al., 2011: 266), alleviating anxiety. And, say the coauthors of this essay, the ability of religious faith to play this vital role is compromised by the mere presence of others with a different worldview. Their very presence is unsettling, threatening, and anxiety-inducing. Mogahed et al. continue as follows:

> Humans' inhumanity to fellow humans is driven by desperate clinging to beliefs, values, and self-esteem as protective shields against the rumble of panic that results from our awareness of the fragile, vulnerable, and temporary nature of human existence ... [People] who see the world differently from how we do, or who don't value us as much as we think we deserve [are] inherently threatening. Rather than face the uncertainty introduced into our lives by a complex and diverse world, we declare the others evil incarnate and struggle to stamp them out. This would be the case – and has been the case – regardless of whether the beliefs and values that divide peoples are sacred or secular, religious or scientific. (Mogahed et al., 2011: 273)

No doubt there is some truth in what these authors are proposing, but some of this is overstated. For a start, outsiders and their ways can be disquieting even if we do not *cling desperately* to our beliefs, values, and so on, but instead endorse them sincerely and calmly, judging them to best account for our circumstances. We may feel that our lives will be the poorer if our beliefs are undermined, and the carriers of the threat may consequently be met with some resistance.

But what really needs to be said in response to this possible objection is twofold. First, many of us spend a lot of time with people whose religious views are very different from ours, and we all know that there are plenty of people out there in the wider world with religious perspectives that greatly differ from ours, and we hardly think of ourselves as threatened by, or in any way hostile to, all of those others all of the time. It just is not a plausible idea.

Second, the shoe is actually on the other foot in the following respect. Rather than what we have here constituting a serious objection to the views advanced in this section, those views provide a telling rejoinder to the perspective from which the objection is advanced. Others are less of a threat if we approach their perspective as an object of respectful curiosity and when we recognize that their perspective, like ours, is – or sometimes is – the product of people of integrity doing the best they can with respect to management of their beliefs, and when in general the magnanimous outlook is adopted toward them.

2 Other Religions

2.1 Introduction

What are insiders to a religious tradition to say about other religious traditions? Is the world a richer and more interesting place in virtue of their presence? Do other religions deserve to be protected and even appreciated? What about their moral and psychological usefulness? Should religious insiders recognize that one can live a rich and complete human life while belonging to another religion? Are other religions *legitimate* and, if so, in what sense or senses? Might religious insiders reasonably believe that some other religions represent authentic and faithful responses to what insiders take to be the facts of the human religious situation, such as the existence of a religious ultimate of some sort?

For example, in his essay "Jewish Chosenness and Religious Diversity: A Contemporary Approach," Jerome Gellman says that some religions other than Judaism, and certainly other forms of monotheism, reflect an authentic response to God's call to humanity (Gellman, 2016: 35). Gellman's view is that God is calling everyone and wants humanity at large to respond to this call freely and joyfully. He also proposes that other monotheistic religions, at any rate, involve beliefs that have developed in response to this call. In these cases, people have done the best they could to understand and to respond to God's call, given their other beliefs and their cultural context. Even if these religions involve some false beliefs, these false beliefs have been formed in the course of freely responding to God's call. Consequently, in Gellman's view, Jews can usefully probe the spiritual inclinations and religious sensibilities to be found in these other religions, and the religions in question are to be deeply respected.

That there are positive elements in other religions is also proposed by Madigan and Sarrió in their up-to-date discussion of Catholic ideas about this and related matters, "Thinking Outside the Box: Developments in Catholic

Understandings of Salvation." They mention approvingly Pope John Paul II's emphasis on "respect for the presence and activity of the Holy Spirit in non-Christians and in their religions – a presence and activity which is seen above all in their practice of virtue, their spirituality and their prayer" (Madigan and Sarrió, 2016: 104).

Constructive elements in other religions might be understood to benefit members of those other religions. Or such elements in those religions might be thought to benefit *insiders*, which is to say members of the religion from within which this judgment about other religions is being made. Indeed, Gellman gestures at this idea when he proposes that Jews can usefully probe the spiritual inclinations and religious sensibilities to be found in various other religions. Gavin D'Costa develops somewhat similar ideas, with a focus on how what is to be learned from others can serve as a basis for questioning and judging ourselves (D'Costa, 1990).

Insiders might benefit in other ways. For example, other religions might be thought to help religious insiders to understand better or to articulate more fully or to appreciate more deeply or to appropriate more thoroughly what they already believe. Thus Madigan and Sarrió find within *Dominus Iesus*, the most recent systematic declaration on these matters from within the Catholic Church, the idea that Christians "can be helped by the activity of the Spirit beyond the Church, and by the presence of 'seeds of the Word' in other traditions, to realize ever more fully what has already been expressed in Christ but not yet fully appropriated. [Other] religious traditions . . . can assist Christians toward a fuller appreciation of the one truth. [Elements in other religions] can also prepare Christians to hear the Gospel more thoroughly" (Madigan and Sarrió, 2016: 78, 79).

Might some of the beliefs associated with other religious traditions be *true*? For example, in his essay "Christian Approaches to the Salvation of Non-Christians," John Sanders draws attention to Christian perspectives according to which all truth is "God's truth," including truths to be found in other religions, truths that can in addition play a salvific role in the lives of adherents of those religions (Sanders, 2016: 135ff.). So, in this case, what is proposed is not only that some beliefs of others are considered true; in addition, some of their beliefs *that have a bearing on their salvation* are considered true.

Perhaps most important of all, what are insiders to say about the *salvific efficacy* of other religions, which is to say their capacity to make salvation possible? For example, Madigan and Sarrió mention that "Christianity and the World Religions," a document issued in 1997 by the International Theological Commission, an international advisory committee of Catholic theologians, states that "one cannot exclude the possibility that [other religions] exercise *as such* a certain salvific function; that is, … they help men achieve their ultimate end" (Madigan and Sarrió, 2016: 106). The view of Madigan and Sarrió is also that when other religions have this capacity to help people achieve their ultimate end, they derive it from processes that Christians uniquely understand and that are intimately associated with Christianity. I shortly turn to this issue of the salvific efficacy of other religions.

Actually while discussing in Section 1 the status of religious others, I have already made some observations about the religions to which those others belong. This is not surprising. If, as proposed in Section 1, we should be pleased by the thought that the distinctive cultural forms of religious others will continue to flourish, this is in effect to say that we should be pleased by the thought that *their traditions* will continue to flourish. And to be curious about religious others – about, say, their history, ideas, customs, relevant experiences, or sacred texts – is to be curious about them *as* members of another religion and hence about that religion. However, in this section, I focus mainly on other religions as such, probing some aspects of what we might say about them. I also include some discussion of what we might say about ourselves in virtue of their presence and, more broadly, how we should react, given their presence.

2.2 The Salvific Efficacy of Other Religions

Discussions of the salvific efficacy of other religions, which is to say the capacity of other religions to make salvation possible, typically invoke a three-part classificatory scheme of exclusivism, inclusivism, and pluralism.[6] Indeed, a three-part analysis along these lines is also widely used to categorize responses to the closely related issue of whether the claims of other religions might be true, a matter I shortly probe. In addition, a three-part analysis of this sort is used to categorize assessments of the salvific status of others, an even more closely related issue, and one to which I turn in the next section.

Wherever they are deployed, exclusivism and pluralism are best understood as two ends of a spectrum with inclusivism in between.[7] I understand *exclusivism* in the matter of the salvific efficacy of other religions to be the view that

---

[6] I use the term "salvation" in this context to refer to all of the accounts of the ideal future state for human beings (or for other beings such as nonhuman animals if they too are capable of salvation) that are proposed by religious traditions. So "salvation" is shorthand for enlightenment, liberation from rebirth, *moksha*, entering the Pure Land, heaven, *samadhi, nirvana, satori*, union with God, and more besides. At least this is so unless I am expositing the views about salvation that are espoused by, say, some scholar or tradition, in which case I may be assuming their notion of salvation.

[7] This and the next few paragraphs draw on the extended discussion of these matters in McKim (2012), especially chapters 4, 5, and 6, in the course of which I consider variations on these options and some examples.

other traditions entirely lack salvific efficacy in the sense that our tradition, the home tradition, alone delivers salvation. It is, or it has associated with it, the sole mechanism of salvation.

Some advocates of exclusivism in this matter of the salvific efficacy of other religions, so defined, say that outsiders or some outsiders can achieve salvation. But according to exclusivists in this matter, they can do so only via the home tradition. Of course there are other advocates of exclusivism, so understood, who say that no outsiders can achieve salvation; they are, in effect, *doubly* exclusivist.

Exclusivists in the matter of the salvific efficacy of other religions of the former type – that is, those who say that outsiders or some outsiders can achieve salvation via the home tradition – will normally have views about conditions that outsiders must satisfy if they are to do so, just as they will normally have views about conditions that would exclude outsiders from doing so. Thus a standard move in theistic traditions is to argue that responding appropriately to whatever truths one has encountered even while being an outsider is necessary if an outsider is to achieve salvation. Another standard move – and here we consider a condition that is understood to exclude someone from salvation – is to argue that anyone who has explicitly *rejected* the message of the home tradition is excluded from salvation. In Section 3, I address this question: are there conditions in which rejection of a message would *reasonably* exclude one from salvation?

Pluralism in the matter of the salvific efficacy of other religions is best understood to say that our religion provides a very viable means to salvation, that many other traditions do equally well, and that no tradition does better than our tradition in this respect. As with pluralism in other areas, pluralism in this matter has it that the traditions in question are on a par in the relevant respect.

And *inclusivism* in this matter of the salvific efficacy of other religions occupies a middle ground between these two alternatives. On one hand, it rejects the exclusivist idea that the home tradition alone makes salvation possible. It says that, contrary to exclusivism in this matter, there are many routes to salvation. On the other hand, it also rejects the pluralist idea that there are other religions that are on a par with the home religion when it comes to delivering salvation. Contrary to pluralism, inclusivism in this matter of the salvific efficacy of other religions says that in one important respect or another that bears on salvation, the home tradition is superior to the competition. This putative superiority can take various forms. Thus the idea might be that other traditions derive from the home tradition whatever capacity they have to deliver salvation. Or the idea might be that the home tradition facilitates the achievement of a superior form of salvation. Again, the idea might be that, while they can deliver salvation, other religions do so less well than the home tradition – a proposal that, if spelled out fully, will require an account of what delivering salvation less well would consist in. Or the idea may be that other traditions can deliver salvation, but this is because they are aimed at a salvific goal that is associated in some special way with the home tradition. In one way or another, the parity claim that is distinctive of pluralism is rejected by each of these variants of inclusivism, each of which nevertheless acknowledges the salvific efficacy of other religions.

A closely related idea that falls short of salvific inclusivism, as defined, is that while other traditions do not provide distinct routes to salvation, they, or some of them, can play a preparatory or a contributing role. Thus Keith Ward, a Christian philosopher and theologian, writes as follows: "Buddhists do not attain Christian salvation, since their Way does not lead to that personal relationship with God which is salvation. They attain a high degree of compassion and inner peace; and their unselfish devotion to the truth as they see it will surely fit them to receive salvation from a personal God when his saving activity becomes clear to them" (Ward, 1990: 16). Again, we find in *Dominus Iesus* the remark that "prayers and rituals of the other religions may assume a role of preparation for the Gospel, in that they are occasions or pedagogical helps in which the human heart is prompted to be open to the action of God" (*Dominus Iesus*, section 21). And I noted earlier the mention by Madigan and Sarrió of the idea that other religions "[may] help men achieve their ultimate end" – a phrase that may point to a range of possibilities, including cases in which a contributory salvific role is played.

In these examples of ways in which a salvific contribution might be made, the beneficiaries are understood to be members of the tradition or traditions that have a capacity to play this contributory role. Another possibility, though, is that those resources might so contribute in the case of the salvific prospects of people who are not members of the traditions in question, including members of the home tradition, which is to say the tradition from which a judgment about the salvific efficacy of other religions is being made. The latter possibility may be hinted at in the remark from Madigan and Sarrió that "[elements in other religions] can also prepare Christians to hear the Gospel more thoroughly" (Madigan and Sarrió, 2016: 79).

The idea of making a salvific contribution is an inclusivistic motif. Other traditions can remove obstacles to salvation or can help with the achievement of salvation in one way or another. Perhaps they help to cultivate character traits or dispositions that make for receptivity to whatever actually secures salvation.

Maybe they provide encouragement; maybe they provide access to important relevant truths and insights. Perhaps they provide such benefits to outsiders or to insiders or to both. What is clear is that there are many ways in which other traditions might be thought to facilitate the salvific process – many ways in which they might make a salvific contribution – even if they are not understood to provide routes to salvation, which is to say, to possess salvific efficacy, as defined.

2.3 The Teachings of Other Religions

Might some of the beliefs associated with other religions be true? As mentioned, in this area too the aforementioned three-part analysis is routinely deployed, though there is considerable variation in how each option is characterized. Perhaps exclusivism in this area is best understood as consisting in something like this combination: our beliefs, or most of them, are true; while other traditions may have some true beliefs, such as beliefs they share with us, we have more true beliefs than any other group, and the beliefs of others – at least their beliefs about important religious matters – are generally false.[8]

Pluralism in this area is, I think, best understood along these lines: a number of religious traditions, including ours, score extremely highly in terms of truth, which is to say that most of their beliefs are true. They also score equally highly in this regard. At least, this is how all-purpose pluralism in this area is best understood. For there is also topic-specific pluralism, according to which most of their beliefs *about a particular topic or area of inquiry* are true. Thus, according to pluralism with respect to a putative religious ultimate, a number of religions are on a par in terms of the truth of their beliefs in this particular area. On this view, the members of those religions are, unbeknownst to themselves and in spite of appearances to the contrary, describing correctly the same religious ultimate, so that the religions in question are on a par in terms of the truth of their beliefs in this area. Someone who is a pluralist with respect to one topic may well be something else – say, an exclusivist or an inclusivist – with respect to other topics. And pluralism of this sort, be it specific to some topic or more general, is very controversial. One obvious reason this is so is that the religions look for all the world as if they contradict each other to a great extent.

According to someone who contends that the beliefs of many religious traditions are equally true – whether this claim is about all areas of inquiry or limited to some particular area, or areas, of inquiry – one can look to the other relevant religious traditions to supplement the account of reality offered by any

---

[8] This and the next few paragraphs draw on my extended discussion of these matters in McKim (2012: chapters 2, 3, and 6).

single tradition, thereby arriving at an account that is more complete than that proposed by any particular tradition.

John Hick is the best-known recent advocate of pluralism with respect to a putative religious ultimate. He refers to the ultimate that he posits as "the Real." Central to Hick's pluralistic hypothesis – as he calls it – is a distinction between the Real as it is in itself and the Real as variously encountered, experienced, and understood by different human communities. Hick proposes that we can say nothing about the Real as it is in itself. At least we can say nothing substantive about it as it is in itself, nothing that provides any significant information about it. We can only say trivial, relatively uninformative things about it, such as that we can say nothing substantive about it. Hick's view is that our substantive concepts and terms – terms such as "person," "thing," "entity," "substance," "process," "good," "evil," "purposive," and "nonpurposive" – do not even apply to it as it is in itself. So, according to Hick, it is not just that we do not know or cannot be sure whether the Real, as it is in itself, is personal or good; the situation is, rather, that the Real as it is in itself is not the sort of thing that could be personal or good or that could possess any such substantive property.

As for the Real as variously encountered, experienced, and understood by different human communities, what Hick proposes is that the Real is encountered by some as God, by others as Allah, by others as Brahman, by others as Nirvana, and so on for the various religious ultimates that are posited by the various religions that are within the scope of his hypothesis. And the religions that are within the scope of his hypothesis are those that have a capacity to reorient people from self-centeredness to Real-centeredness, where this includes altruism. He believes that all of the major global religious traditions have this capacity and that, as far as we can tell, they have it to the same extent. So various substantive concepts do apply to the various personal and impersonal ultimates that are posited by the religions that have this capacity. And these ultimates are the product of interaction between the Real as it is in itself and the various relevant traditions. There is causal input from both of these directions and the various phenomena of religious worship and practice (God, Allah, Krishna, Brahman, Nirvana, and so forth) represent the confluence of these two causal streams.

Questions have been raised about the viability of Hick's distinction between properties that are substantive and those that are trivial; about whether Hick himself actually attributes only trivial properties to the Real; about whether a Real concerning which, as it is in itself, nothing substantive may be said best accounts for the evidence that Hick adduces in support of his hypothesis; about the religious adequacy of his pluralistic hypothesis, and about the viability of his entire proposal. Questions have also been raised about how Hick understands, and should interpret, the relationship between the Real as it is in itself and the Real as variously encountered, experienced, and understood: indeed how this relationship is understood has a bearing on whether Hick actually is a pluralist with respect to what is religiously ultimate, as this view has been defined earlier in this section. (There is a sizeable literature on these topics. For some discussion, see, e.g., Quinn, 2000; Eddy, 2002; Tuggy, 2015; McKim, 2012: chapter 6.)

Still, whatever its deficiencies, Hick's proposal is a bold initiative that is underpinned both by formidable learning and by an admirable appreciation of the traditions of others. If you think, as I do, that it is not viable in the form in which he presented it, the question arises whether there might be a modified version of it that is viable. Certainly a viable pluralistic proposal remains a possibility and investigation of this possibility is an important field of inquiry. Maybe new pluralistic proposals will emerge that will be worth taking seriously. (For an introduction to some options, see Tuggy, 2015.) Maybe such proposals will need to be fashioned on the anvil of forms of religious participation that have not yet been developed and that we cannot currently envisage.

Inclusivism with respect to this matter of whether the beliefs of others might be true is best thought of as occupying a middle ground between exclusivism and pluralism.[9] Probably inclusivism in this area is best thought of along these lines: others have many true beliefs, some of which may overlap with ours and some of which may be truths of their own, and in this area we are only somewhat better off than others.

There are also some interesting views that are close to pluralism as defined in this section but that are, I think, best understood as forms of inclusivism or perhaps as inclusivist themes: these include the idea that other traditions have important insights into, or interesting perspectives on, some religiously significant matter such as the character of a religious ultimate.

Consider this. A tree might be seen in terms of its value to its ecosystem and as something that sustains numerous other forms of life; an ecologist or biologist might see it thus. A physicist might see the tree in terms of its fundamental constituents, as these are currently understood in physics. An investor might see it in terms of the monetary value of its timber; a carpenter might see it in terms of what sort of furniture could be made from

---

[9] Some have questioned the usefulness of the term "inclusivism," and, indeed, the relevance of the familiar trichotomy of options, in this matter of the truth of the teachings of other traditions. Eddy (2016), passim and especially 191–192, has some helpful discussion of the issues. My view is just that there is a range of significantly different options here and we need some way to refer to them.

it given its quality and dimensions; a person who deals in property might see something that enhances the value of the property on which the tree is growing; a gardener might see the tree as providing shade that will protect various crops in summer. Perhaps it is a tree under which a family tragedy of some sort occurred and it will long be recalled by family members as the tree under which that traumatic event occurred. And so on.

These possibilities vary in many ways. For example, some seem to be about the tree itself whereas others seem to be about the relationship between the tree and other things. What the examples mentioned indicate, though, is the possibility of manifold somewhat informative perspectives on the same reality. Probably the view under discussion is best understood as pluralistic only if the perspectives in question are taken to be *equally* informative and insightful. If others are talking about the same reality that we are talking about but their grasp of it is inferior to ours, probably this is best understood as an inclusivistic motif.

In any case, many variations exist on this theme of there being a variety of insights into a significant religious matter. Perhaps some other traditions merely have long-term potential for coming up with such insights but have not yet managed to do so.

It is beyond my present purposes to provide a thorough assessment of all of the options mentioned. However, broadly speaking, inclusivistic attitudes seem especially promising, at least in the areas I have focused on, namely truth and salvation. Pluralism is difficult to defend, not least because parity across the traditions is just one of a vast number of alternatives: we would need a compelling argument to the effect that there *is* parity; in addition, attempts to articulate pluralistic proposals have not to date proven convincing. At least, all of this is so in the case of pluralism about salvation and about what is true. (One might be a pluralist about various other matters. Thus one might be a pluralist with respect to the capacity of a number of religions to reorient people from self-centeredness to Real-centeredness, to use Hick's terms, believing that a number of religions are equally effective in this regard; Hick himself was a pluralist of this sort.)

Exclusivism, on the other hand, is *troubling* to defend.[10] So in general I favor inclusivistic options, though, as I say, I do not presume to try to settle such complex and difficult matters here. Instead, I next introduce additional reflections about how we should think about other religions.

---

[10] I say a little about some of the difficulties that arise for salvific exclusivism in McKim (2012: 64ff).

2.4 An Appropriate Attitude to Other Religions

As intimated at the end of Section 1, to endorse the magnanimous outlook toward religious others is in effect to endorse much the same outlook to the religions of those others. So we can carry over many of the elements introduced in the context of thinking about magnanimity toward religious others, identifying corresponding elements in the case of other religions. This would include seeing the religions as having developed under religiously ambiguous circumstances, taking an exploratory and courteous approach to them, being curious about them, and being willing to learn from them. However, some ideas come to the fore when we adopt this attitude to other religions as such.

For one thing, we can acknowledge that the world is a richer and more interesting place on account of the presence of a variety of religious traditions just as it is richer and more interesting in virtue of linguistic, cultural, and biological diversity. In addition, a variety of perspectives provides people with an opportunity to choose among them. Each religious tradition typically has associated with it various ideals, diverse accounts of what makes for a worthwhile life, and an account of what character traits and dispositions should be cultivated. A broader array of traditions makes a broader array of such resources available. And the lives of those who have the option of choosing among a variety of religious perspectives are richer, all other things being equal.

However, the magnanimous outlook does not assume that other traditions are on a par with our tradition in terms of being, say, equally true or equally effective salvifically, or equally morally inspiring, or the like. Someone who is magnanimous in the relevant sense may endorse some such pluralistic ideas, but the magnanimous outlook as such does not commit one to this.

Moreover, it is consistent with everything I have said that there are religious traditions that are so far *below par* in one or another important respect that they do not merit the magnanimous approach. For example, it might be that it appears that the relevant beliefs are *not* held by people of integrity and have *not* had a central place in enduring cultures whose members include many such people. Or the character traits and dispositions encouraged within the group across its long history may seem unimpressive. Or the founders or current leaders may show every sign of being frauds or crooks or liars.

I do not have a full proposal about how many traditions, and which traditions, should be at the receiving end of the magnanimous approach. For example, should we include only those associated with major historically significant religious traditions? What about agnosticism and atheism? And should we include only traditions that continue to be major players on the world stage? And so on. A full proposal would provide answers to these and many more questions. In addition, we have no way to specify with any precision the threshold beneath which a tradition would be disqualified from deserving to be treated with magnanimity and a full proposal would address the various relevant indicators.

But we can make a few points in this area. First, we can be confident that major religious traditions that have stood the test of time and that are established across large populations with diverse backgrounds and varying levels of educational achievement are above the relevant threshold. Second, in considering other traditions in this context, we probably should consider them at their best; certainly we should not consider them at their worst. (*We* – whoever we may be – do not look good at our worst.) Indeed, in reflecting about this matter, we should consider other religions in a somewhat idealized fashion. What I have in mind here is nicely exemplified by an aspect of William P. Alston's discussion of how best to handle apparent discrepancies between, on one hand, various Christian beliefs that are formed in response to various religious experiences and, on the other hand, the findings of science:

> Even if some scientific results should contradict something central to the Christian faith, the question would remain as to whether that faith could be reconstructed so as to be compatible with the result in question and still be definitively Christian. After all, the faith has undergone many such modifications in the past. Today most Christians are inclined to think that the features that were discarded or changed were not essential to the faith, but that is a retrospective judgment. They seemed essential to many at the time, and perhaps an analogous fate is in store for some features that seem essential to us today. (Alston, 1991: 241)

I would just add that the reconstruction might be called for not only because of scientific developments. For example, a better understanding of other faiths and more information about them might also make clear a need for such modifications.

Third, if there are entire traditions whose status is uncertain so that it is unclear whether they are "in" or "out," surely there are some that clearly are "in." Even if there are, say, *five*, or even *three*, traditions that are clearly above the relevant threshold, that itself is an extremely important conclusion to come to; to extend the appropriate attitude to those traditions we so classify might occupy all of our spare time. Fourth, even in the case of a tradition that does not qualify for this response, the magnanimous outlook is still *relevant*. For one thing, *some elements* of the magnanimous outlook may remain appropriate: thus a courteous interest in that tradition and curiosity about it may be appropriate. In general, we should implement as much of the magnanimous outlook as is appropriate. We can also recognize that it would be better if a group *were* deserving of the magnanimous outlook and there may be steps we can take to encourage that development.

We should think of the promotion of magnanimity, both in the case of religious others and in the case of other religions, as a *program* – a program that both individuals and religious traditions can engage in. Magnanimity in this context is often difficult: it is all too easy, especially in contexts in which there are tensions or conflict, to be less than magnanimous. Thinking of the in-group as superior and as the people who really matter, and of the out-group as inferior and mattering less, if it matters at all, can come naturally and be part of how situations and encounters are automatically interpreted, even by people who are generally well intentioned. (Who among us has not encountered this phenomenon?) Magnanimity requires effort, perseverance, and self-scrutiny. Institutional support may be necessary for its achievement, and this is in effect to raise the question of whether new institutions might be needed to promote and encourage it.

2.5 Other Religions and the Home Religion

What are religious insiders to say about the home tradition itself in light of the presence of other traditions and in light of our acquaintance with their members and with their views? Actually, a good deal has already been said about some aspects of this issue. For one thing, to believe that other traditions are, say, on a par with us in some respect is to believe that we are on a par with them in that respect. Again, to believe that other traditions, or some other traditions, are salvifically effective and that they derive their salvific effectiveness from our religion is also to believe something important about our religion.

And how should we think of *ourselves*, and of our practices, salvific status, historical significance, and so on, in light of the presence of others, and in virtue of saying whatever it is we think we should say about them? Is there a correct way to respond to their presence? Should we modify our beliefs, or modify how we hold them, in virtue of the presence of others who disagree with us? How does the caliber of those who disagree with us bear on this issue? Some such questions, by the way, arise too for entirely secular individuals: in their case, one question that arises is what sort of challenge the presence of various religions constitutes for them.

Some forms of enrichment are facilitated by contact with others. In thinking about this, I have found helpful some work by Alasdair MacIntyre. MacIntyre's concern in this work is with the value of competing large-scale *intellectual* traditions, and his particular concern is with Thomas Aquinas's attempt to accommodate both the Aristotelian and the Augustinian traditions. Among the benefits of competing intellectual traditions, he says, is the fact that each can "ask whether the alternative and rival traditions may not be able to provide resources to characterize and to explain the failings and defects of their own tradition more adequately than they, using the resources of [their own] tradition, have been able to do" (MacIntyre, 1988: 167). MacIntyre says that a "rare gift of empathy as well as of intellectual insight" is needed "to be able to understand the theses, arguments, and concepts of their rival in such a way that they are able to view themselves from such an alien standpoint and to recharacterize their own beliefs in an appropriate manner from the alien perspective of the rival tradition" (167). Naturally, I am interested in the application of these ideas in the context of thinking about competing *religious* traditions. A crucial point here is just that the availability of other perspectives can help us to see ourselves – our perspective, our history, our defects, but also our strengths and accomplishments – as others see us, and this can be instructive. (Gavin D'Costa explores ideas along these lines within a Christian Trinitarian framework (D'Costa, 1990: 23ff.)) Indeed, when you think of it, the religions pay strikingly little attention to the value of seeing ourselves as others see us. It almost seems as if they are structured so as to obscure this sort of insight.

2.6 Steps That Might Be Taken in Response to the Presence of Other Religions

Some scholars contend that the appropriate response to the challenge provided to religions that have a central place for belief by the presence of other religions is to engage in a process of reflection and examination. In a recent essay, "The Role of Religious Diversity in Meaningful Religious Belief Assessment: One Professor's Experience," David Basinger advances this thesis and probes some of its pedagogical implications:

> When people are aware that apparently sincere and knowledgeable individuals affirm perspectives on a religious issue that are significantly different from the perspective they affirm, they should engage in comparative belief assessment. (Basinger, 2016: passim)

Comparative belief assessment, as Basinger defines it, requires attempting to identify the reasons each of the disagreeing parties has for its beliefs, giving serious consideration to the various relevant sets of reasons, and then attempting to determine whether one remains justified in continuing to affirm one's current perspective or whether one is required to modify this perspective in some way. Basinger's view is that this sort of assessment leads to belief clarification and can result in belief refinement or belief replacement.

Engaging in this sort of assessment, he observes, is difficult. For one thing, our beliefs seem, to a considerable extent, to be out of our control. Basinger says – reasonably in my view – that the payoffs of comparative belief assessment will include respectful dialogue, tolerance, and increased understanding. (Basinger 2016: 227–228; see also Basinger, 2002: passim, and especially chapter 2, for views that are broadly consistent with these but that have a different focus.) In earlier work, I have defended the rather similar idea that when there is disagreement of the sort that we find among the religious traditions, parties to the disagreement with the requisite abilities and opportunities ought to examine the relevant beliefs, both their own beliefs and competing beliefs (McKim, 2001: 140; also 146–153 and chapter 9).

Other scholars contend that the best response to the challenge provided to those religions that have a central place for belief by the presence of other religions is to eschew belief as such, substituting one or other of these "propositional attitudes": having faith that various claims are true, hoping that various claims are true, accepting that various claims are true, presuming that various claims are true, or treating various claims as working hypotheses.

Yet others contend that the significance of religious diversity is best registered with such responses as these: not regarding views on a disputed matter as the only rational option, recognizing that some may reasonably reject your views, recognizing that belief in a disputed area involves epistemic risk, or thinking that current formulations of beliefs are approximations and subject to revision.

In earlier work, I have argued that when there is disagreement of the sort that we find among the religious traditions, parties to the disagreement who have the requisite abilities and opportunities ought to hold their relevant beliefs tentatively, where this involves a recognition that you may be mistaken, a willingness to revise your beliefs, an openness to alternative beliefs, and an awareness that some of the competing beliefs may be plausible or even correct (McKim, 2001: 141; also chapters 8 and 9).

2.7 Religious Diversity and Religious Experience

Another interesting area of inquiry is the bearing of religious diversity on the extent to which any religious perspective is justified or appropriate. Consider, for instance, the significance of the fact that diverse religious traditions each have their own history of religious experience. J. L. Schellenberg contends that the diversity of religious experiences constitutes a problem for all attempts to invoke such experience in support of the claims of any particular religious tradition. In his view, this is a barrier to various "innocent until proven guilty" approaches to religious experience, by which is meant roughly the idea that in light of your religious experiences, it is reasonable to continue to hold whatever religious views you hold on the basis of those experiences until given reason to do otherwise (Schellenberg, 2007: 166ff.). An example is the approach William P. Alston advocates in *Perceiving God: The Epistemology of Religious Experience* (Alston, 1991).

For one thing, awareness of the diversity of religious experience should, according to Schellenberg, raise this question for anyone who enjoys such experiences: since the experiences associated with many other religious traditions are not indicative of what is true, maybe my experiences are not either. He says that "[such] questions must have a profoundly cautionary effect" (Schellenberg, 2007: 176). He also observes that whatever our own religious experiences may be, we do not know what we would think if we had access to the private experiences of others. Indeed, he says that since we know we *could* have the religious experiences of many others, and have every reason to believe that if we had their experiences we would come to different conclusions, any justification that would otherwise issue from our own experiences is undermined.

As I see it, Schellenberg is right to this extent: the diversity of forms of religious experience constitutes a problem for "innocent until proven guilty" approaches to religious experience. It imposes additional apologetic burdens. This is, in turn, an instance of a broader truth, namely that religious diversity, as a whole, imposes additional apologetic burdens, requires additional apologetic steps, and should – in Schellenberg's phrase – have a cautionary effect. It is somewhat disruptive of business as usual, religiously speaking. On the other hand, Schellenberg's claims that (a) knowledge that we *could* have the religious experiences of many others and that (b) we have every reason to believe that if we had their experiences, we would come to different conclusions, *undermine* whatever justification would otherwise arise from our own experiences, seems more debatable and may overstate the case. Relevant issues include the clarity of our own experience; the clarity of the experiences of others; whether the relevant experiences – ours and theirs – require skill and judgment for their interpretation and whether we, and they, have this skill and judgment if it is needed; and more besides.

In his essay "A Christian Perspective," Charles Taliaferro suggests that Christians might question whether the religious experiences that are enjoyed in different traditions are as different as they may seem at first glance, which would raise the possibility that they are less of a challenge to each other. However, he is not inclined to press this point. More promising, he proposes, is the strategy of questioning the coherence of concepts deployed by others as they interpret their experiences. He mentions the Buddhist idea of no-self in this context (Taliaferro, 2011: 388; Wainwright, 1988: chapter 7, has an illuminating discussion of much the same issues). This move too seems debatable. No doubt there are non-Christians who would make much the same move in response to Christian appeals to religious experience. And I do not think that doing so would do much to advance debate. Indeed, claims that a particular religion is superior to the competition in terms of the coherence of its concepts are two-a-penny. The concepts of others can easily seem incoherent as well as alien. Needless to say, I do not deny that there are incoherent concepts. And the fact that a concept seems incoherent to us has to be taken seriously. But the thought might occur to me that a concept may seem incoherent to me because it has not been explicated as felicitously as it might have been. Relevant questions include the following. Has the concept in question been articulated in the clearest possible way with the most promising ways of thinking and reasoning deployed in the process? Is this concept currently interwoven with others from which it might profitably be detached? Is the concept deployed in the lives of religious others in ways that cast light on how it is best understood? Has there been reflection – careful, probing, sensitive, helpful, insightful reflection – on the part of the deepest thinkers with relevant expertise about what a coherent rendering of this concepts might amount to? When the issue of coherence is being considered, in addition to the internal coherence of a concept, there is the question of *external* coherence, which is to say the question of what we expect the concept in question to cohere with or, in other words, what beliefs, worldview, and so on we are taking for granted as we probe the coherence of this concept. (For a few relevant thoughts about this last point, see Alston, 1991: 248.)

On the other hand, Taliaferro also makes the irenic comment that "[diversity] should, however, give one reason to reflect on the goods that might be in play in other religions, and it is also a reason to explore whether or not one's own faith is indeed the true faith or the one that is most reasonable" (Taliaferro 2011: 390). This is a signpost that points in a more promising direction.

3 The Salvific Status of Religious Others

3.1 Introduction

What are religious insiders to say about whether outsiders can achieve salvation? If outsiders can achieve salvation, under what conditions can they do so? And under what conditions are they excluded from salvation?

Obviously this matter of the salvific status of outsiders is intimately linked to the issue of the salvific efficacy of other traditions, which was the focus of some discussion in Section 2. For example, to discuss whether other religions can deliver salvation is, in effect, to discuss whether members of those other religions can benefit in this respect from their participation in their religion. So the discussion of Section 2 certainly has a bearing on the salvific prospects of religious others. Moreover, the question of the salvific status of religious others is intimately related to the question of what we say overall about religious others. Hence the discussion of Section 1 is also relevant here. However, interesting issues come to the fore when we focus directly on the question of whether others might achieve salvation.

If we deploy in *this* context the now familiar three-part analysis of exclusivism, inclusivism, and pluralism, the natural approach to take is as follows. Exclusivism in this matter will have it that we alone can achieve salvation. Pluralism, at the other extreme, will have it that we and various others are equally well situated with respect to the achievement of salvation. Inclusivism, occupying an intermediate position, will say that while outsiders can achieve salvation, insiders are better off with respect to the achievement of salvation in some significant way.

As a first step in probing the issues in this area on which I wish to focus, I begin with some ideas from John Sanders, an evangelical Christian philosopher, about how to understand the distinction between inclusivist and exclusivist Christian responses to the question of whether the unevangelized – those who have not encountered the Christian gospel – can achieve salvation. Sanders observes that Christians have generally considered two scriptural teachings especially relevant to the issue of the salvation of non-Christians: the idea that God loves, and desires to save, all sinners; and the idea that it is through Jesus alone that salvation is made available (Sanders, 2016: 121). This includes Christians who are *exclusivists* in this matter of the salvific status of the unevangelized. What distinguishes exclusivists with respect to this matter is the fact that they *also* endorse the view that knowledge of and belief in the gospel of Jesus is necessary for salvation (Sanders, 2016: 123). By "knowledge of and belief in the gospel" I take him to mean two things. First, there is belief (or perhaps knowledge) that the two scriptural teachings are true – or, perhaps, belief in the truth of a larger set of claims that together constitute the gospel and that includes these two teachings. Second, there is *belief in* the gospel of Jesus; later, he refers to this component as "trust in Jesus" (Sanders, 2016: 128). So this second element is a matter of *trusting in*, or *relying on*, as distinct from believing that something is the case. Only Christians will meet these requirements. As indicated, Sanders's view is that both elements are understood by exclusivists of the relevant sort as necessary for salvation.

Sanders understands inclusivism in this context to involve endorsement of the two scriptural teachings and *rejection* of the requirements that have to do with belief – both the *belief that* requirement and the *belief in* requirement. What is necessary, according to inclusivists, is responding favorably to whatever revelation you have received. And he mentions this favorable response in particular: seeking what is true and good, and loving others (Sanders, 2016: 128, 129). So, according to Christian inclusivism so understood, an outsider may be able to achieve salvation in virtue of the truth of the two scriptural teachings and in spite of not meeting either belief requirement provided he or she responds favorably in the specified ways.

However, "seeking what is true and good, and loving others," and in particular *seeking what is true*, seems to involve a requirement that *has to do with* belief. Perhaps the idea is that you must be aiming to have true beliefs or be disposed to have true beliefs. In that case, a belief requirement of a sort is involved here – a somewhat different sort of belief requirement from those mentioned while introducing exclusivism. And this element that has to do with belief is combined with what seems to be a moral requirement, namely seeking what is good and loving others. Much of the focus of this section is on the idea of a belief requirement. As we have just seen, a belief requirement can play a role both in exclusivism and in inclusivism, as defined; I focus mostly on inclusivism, identifying a number of proposals of this sort.

By way of identifying a range of additional inclusivistic ideas in this area, and with a view to introducing the issues to which I wish to pay particular attention, I mention some relevant ideas that surface in the work of Madigan and Sarrió. These authors point out that two elements of the teachings of the Catholic Church have long provided the basis for an inclusive approach to this matter of the salvific status of religious others. The first is the idea of "implicit faith" or an "implicit desire" to enter the Church. "Such implicit faith was sufficient to guarantee a kind of honorary, even if unconscious, membership in the Church" (Madigan and Sarrió, 2016: 94). This move in effect turns some, maybe many, outsiders into quasi-insiders, albeit ones who are unaware of their status. One can see that there are many possible variations on this theme. In particular, there are many possible answers to the question of what the implicit faith or desire consists in. For example, it has been understood to be a matter of a faith in God that lacks specifically Christian elements and that could have been endorsed prior to Christ (Madigan and Sarrió, 2016: 87, 89, 90). And it has been understood to be a matter of desiring God and desiring what God wills (Madigan and Sarrió, 2016: 93, 94).

The second element in Church teaching that, according to Madigan and Sarrió, has long provided a basis for an inclusive approach is the idea of "invincible ignorance." This, they say, is "ignorance in the literal sense of not knowing something, and invincible in the sense that, through no fault of one's own, there is no possibility of coming to know it" (Madigan and Sarrió, 2016: 94). Madigan and Sarrió quote with approval remarks from Pope John Paul II that bespeak considerable optimism about the salvation of people outside of the Church, and that are intended to pertain in particular to the "invincibly ignorant": "For such people salvation in Christ is accessible by virtue of a grace which, while having a mysterious relationship to the Church, does not make them formally part of the Church but enlightens them in a way which is accommodated to their spiritual and material situation. This grace comes from Christ; it is the result of his Sacrifice and is communicated by the Holy Spirit. It enables each person to attain salvation through his or her free cooperation (*Redemptoris missio*, n. 10)" (Madigan and Sarrió, 2016: 95). What this second element adds is the idea that salvation would be available to people who *through no fault of their own* lack what is normally required for salvation. (Indeed, I wonder if this second element might be better referred to as *inculpable* ignorance. "Invincible" suggests it cannot be overcome. But surely those who endorse this idea believe that the ignorance in question could be overcome – for example, by direct divine intervention.)

Madigan and Sarrió also draw special attention to various ideas that, in their view, have increasingly and appropriately been the focus of attention in Catholic discussions of the salvation of outsiders, including the ideas of *health* and of *orientation*. As employed by these scholars, these too are inclusivistic ideas. They characterize a healthy life as one that is "creative, compassionate, loving, faithful, honest and generous" (Madigan and Sarrió, 2016: 99). They reasonably observe that it "would be foolhardy to maintain that outside the Church no one is healthy in the fully human sense. We can observe all around us people leading admirably healthy human lives" (Madigan and Sarrió, 2016: 99). Indeed they say that "this salvation, this health . . . may at times be lacking within the Church and be in evidence beyond its borders" (Ibid.)

As for the idea of orientation, Madigan and Sarrió note that the Church has come to appreciate the fact that many non-Catholics are oriented as the Church is oriented. In a passage I quoted at the start of this Element they write that the outsiders in question are "in effect facing, striving even, in the same direction – desiring the same justice, love and peace that are to be the hallmarks of the Reign of God" (Madigan and Sarrió, 2016: 101).

However, Madigan and Sarrió also propose that "[what] makes for a healthy, fully human life, Christians claim, is living at one with God, at home with God, at table with God, sharing in the divine life. This we are enabled to do because of God's initiative in irreversibly binding God's own self to humanity, something we claim to have witnessed God doing decisively in Jesus Christ" (Madigan and Sarrió, 2016: 99). And they attribute to Pope Pius IX the idea that "the salvation of those outside the Church, when it happens, [is] the effect of 'divine light and grace' acting in the hearts of the individuals" (Madigan and Sarrió, 2016: 99). Moreover, they report with approval the judgment of the International Theological Commission that outsiders who are correctly oriented "are so not by chance but because of the action of God's spirit, often in and through the positive elements of their religious traditions" (Madigan and Sarrió, 2016: 106). The upshot is that the *explanation* of an orientation to justice, love, and peace, when it occurs, and of a fully healthy life of the relevant sort, when it occurs, is that these arise from a certain sort of relationship to God – even when the people involved have no inkling that this is so. Hence a fully healthy life and a correctly oriented life have elements that can *properly be understood* only from a Christian perspective; this is so because factors uniquely associated with Christianity are understood to have played a crucial causal role.

So far we have seen a number of variations on these distinctive inclusivist elements: while outsiders can achieve salvation, insiders are better off with respect to the achievement of salvation in one or another respect. For example, the salvific process required for salvation to occur is understood to be uniquely associated with the insiders' tradition. Or only the insiders' tradition understands what is going on when salvation occurs.

Moreover – to turn to the issue I want to pursue in most detail – salvific inclusivism will always have something to say about the conditions that outsiders must meet if they are to achieve salvation. In the examples considered, the conditions mentioned have to do either with belief or with moral requirements. The moral requirements seem relatively uncomplicated, at least in broad outline. According to Christian inclusivism, as described by Sanders, whether one loves others is a salient consideration. According to the contemporary Catholic Christian perspective that is both described and advocated by Madigan and Sarrió, living a life that is "creative, compassionate, loving, faithful, honest and generous" and being oriented toward justice, love, and peace are salient considerations. A statement of these requirements is uncomplicated and straightforward. Fulfilling such requirements in your life is another matter entirely and, needless to say, it is often no easy task. Who among us can claim to be successful in this regard? In what follows, I pay particular attention to requirements that have to do with belief.

3.2 Belief Requirements and the Salvific Status of Outsiders

As we have seen, sometimes there is understood to be a requirement having to do with belief that outsiders must satisfy if they are to be eligible for salvation.

Correspondingly, an outsider who fails to satisfy that requirement is understood to be ineligible for salvation. Can we make sense of such a requirement? And who could reasonably be held accountable for not believing? Does it make sense to think that a failure in the area of belief could be salvifically catastrophic?

For example, the idea may be that people who are presented with a particular message or communication – one or more beliefs that have been communicated to them – and who fail to believe are ineligible for salvation. In that case, outsiders can achieve salvation only if the relevant beliefs have not been communicated to them. Or the idea might be that people to whom the beliefs in question have been presented *in a particular way* and who fail to respond appropriately are ineligible for salvation. The particular way in question – the way in which the beliefs would need to be presented to them – might be understood as a matter of being exposed to a convincing case for those beliefs. In that case, outsiders can achieve salvation only if they have not been exposed to a convincing case for the teachings of the insiders' tradition. (Sometimes options such as those mentioned in this paragraph are presented with an additional twist. This is the idea that what matters is not that a person actually believes or fails to believe, or actually believes or fails to believe under certain circumstances. Rather, what determines eligibility for salvation is what he or she *would* believe or fail to believe if he or she *were* in the relevant circumstances.)

I am especially interested in what a *plausible* and *satisfactory* view in this area might amount to, and in whether any such view is plausible and satisfactory. For one thing, such a view would need to be realistic in the sense of not holding people accountable for, say, believing things they could not reasonably be expected to believe – for example, because they have not been given adequate reason to believe them. I probe further some possibilities in this area by considering some recent work on Islamic forms of salvific inclusivism and on issues raised by this work.

Mohammad Hassan Khalil characterizes salvific inclusivism as the view that salvation may be attained by sincere and righteous non-Muslims who, for whatever reason, could not have been expected to recognize the truth of Muhammad's message (Khalil, 2016: 149). This is an interpretation of inclusivism as it pertains to the main issue under discussion in this section, namely the salvific status of outsiders, in this case, outsiders to Islam. Interestingly, Khalil proposes that salvific inclusivism, so understood, has been the "dominant soteriological paradigm ... among exegetes, theologians, and mystics" throughout most of Islamic history (Khalil, 2016: 150–151). He distinguishes three rather different versions of salvific inclusivism, so understood, within Islam, and he locates these on a spectrum from *limited* to *liberal* inclusivism. Khalil starts with an exposition of the "limited inclusivism" of medieval Syrian theologian Ibn Taymiyya. According to Ibn Taymiyya, there is no salvation for the "reached" who reject Islam. This is because, in his view, sincere and righteous non-Muslims who encounter Muhammad's message and miracles *cannot but submit* to his religion. "Submission is the only response that accords with a disposition of righteousness" (Khalil, 2016: 152). Hence, if the reached reject Islam, it follows that they are at fault, lacking sincerity or righteousness, for example. Khalil classifies Ibn Taymiyya as a *limited* inclusivist because while Ibn Taymiyya allows that non-Muslims can achieve salvation, he says that only non-Muslims who have not been reached by the message of Islam can do so.

People who do not encounter Islam fall into two categories, according to Ibn Taymiyya. First, there are "People of the Book," who, being aware of their respective scriptures, have some exposure to revelation. People in this category are tested in terms of whether they have sincerely pursued whatever truth is accessible to them. Second, the completely unreached will be tested by a messenger on Judgment Day. So the non-Muslims who can achieve salvation, in addition to not having been reached by the message of Islam, belong to either of these categories: first, there are those who have encountered *some* revelation and have responded appropriately to what they have encountered, where this appropriate response presumably involves acquiring various beliefs; second, there are those who pass whatever test is imposed by a messenger on Judgment Day.

Next, Khalil considers a form of salvific inclusivism that is endorsed by al-Ghazali, a medieval Persian theologian (Khalil, 2016: 156ff.). Ghazali distinguishes three groups of non-Muslims:

(1) the unreached who have never even heard the name "Muhammad,"
(2) those who know of the Prophet and his character and nevertheless arrogantly or negligently reject his message, and
(3) those who have heard only falsehoods about Muhammad. (Khalil, 2016: 156)

Khalil writes as follows of Ghazali's views: "[Both] the first and third categories of non-Muslims are eligible to receive divine clemency – despite their problematic creeds … The second group, however, are culpable because they came to learn of Muhammad's character, miracles, and message, yet closed their minds to his truth claims" (Khalil, 2016: 156).

Khalil says that Ghazali also, in effect, identifies a fourth group of non-Muslims: sincere non-Muslim truth-seekers who will be saved despite being among the reached. It seems that these people are actively investigating Islam and are *not* arrogantly or negligently rejecting the message of Islam. But they have not yet been convinced of its truth (Khalil, 2016: 157). Ghazali is in effect making space salvifically for some non-Muslims who would be excluded by Ibn Taymiyya, namely seekers after truth who have been reached but have not yet made up their minds.

The "liberal inclusivism" of medieval Andalusian mystic Ibn Arabi is the third option to which Khalil draws attention. Ibn Arabi's interpretation of "We do not chastise until We have sent a messenger" (Quran 17:15) is central to Khalil's classification of him as a *liberal* inclusivist (Khalil, 2016: 154ff.). Here is how Ibn Arabi interprets this passage:

> Note that [God] did not say, "[We do not punish] until We [have sent] a person." Hence the *message* of the one who is sent must be established for the one to whom it is directed. There must be clear and manifest proofs established for each person to whom the messenger is sent, for many a sign has within it obscurity or equivocality such that some people do not perceive what it proves. The clarity of the proof must be such that it establishes the person's [messengership] for each person to whom he is sent. Only then, if the person refuses it, will he/she be taken to account. Hence, this verse has within it a tremendous mercy, because of the diversity of human dispositions that lead to a diversity of views. He who knows the all-inclusiveness of the divine mercy, which God reports, [*encompasses*] *all things* [Quran 7:156], knows that God did this only because of mercy toward His servants.[11]

Ibn Arabi's view is along these lines: only someone who is provided with a proof of various Islamic claims and then refuses to hold the relevant beliefs will be rendered ineligible for salvation by his or her non-belief. Maybe such a person must in addition actually have been *convinced* by those proofs. I shortly consider various options in this area, asking which of them Ibn Arabi seems to have in mind and, more important, whether any of them is plausible.

The difference between Ghazali and Ibn Arabi, a difference that Khalil reasonably takes to render the former less liberal than the latter, is along the following lines. Ghazali says that those who are acquainted with the Prophet and his character and yet arrogantly or negligently reject his message will be punished. Ibn Arabi says that those who are acquainted with the Prophet *via proofs that suffice to convince them* – or something along these lines – and yet

---

[11] Ibn al-'Arabī, *al-Futūḥāt al-makkiyyah* (Beirut: Dār Sādir, [1968]), 3:469. Quoted at Mohammad Hassan Khalil (2016: 154–155).

culpably reject his message will be punished. The latter view seems more liberal or, if you will, more inclusive.

At least the latter view seems more liberal provided that those in Ghazali's second category – those who know of the Prophet and his character and nevertheless arrogantly or negligently reject his message – are assumed to have become acquainted with the Prophet in some way that falls short of their being provided with the sort of proof that Ibn Arabi has in mind, and if in addition we assume a rough equivalence between the modes in which these scholars are envisioning the rejection to occur: in the one case, "arrogantly or negligently," and, in the other case, "culpably." So we have before us a number of statements of salvific inclusivism that involve a belief requirement. Next I want to probe further some of these options.

3.3 Are There Reasonable Belief Requirements?

One approach that should be summarily rejected is Ibn Taymiyya's limited inclusivism. Given religious ambiguity as defined in Section 1, Ibn Taymiyya's position is implausible. Contrary to what he proposes, sincere and righteous people – on any plausible interpretation of "sincere" and "righteous" – embrace all manner of conclusions about religious matters. Simply put, there is no religious perspective such that sincere and righteous people who encounter it will inevitably endorse it.

On the other hand, the remarks quoted earlier from Ibn Arabi, and in which he provides an interpretation of the Quranic remark that "We do not chastise until We have sent a messenger," provide a more promising starting point for reflection. However, in order to pin down the salient issues here, I want to set aside an aspect of what Ibn Arabi is talking about in this passage. According to Ibn Arabi, *two* things apparently need to be established (in some way we have yet to clarify) if nonbelief is to render one ineligible for salvation: on one hand, the messengership of the messenger and, on the other hand, the message as such.

These are different. For one thing, if a "clear and manifest" proof of the message as such were available, then the message would seem to stand alone in the sense that there is every reason to believe it, irrespective of *who* has made this proof available. Or at any rate there could be cases of this sort.

In addition there is the question of whether *everything* said by a messenger whose prophethood has been established should thereby be understood to have been established. A messenger might make a casual observation about, say, the weather or the price of a cup of tea at a local market or about any matter at all but not, so to speak, be wearing a prophetic hat while making that observation.

Hence the messengership of someone might be established and yet it might not be clear that something he or she said was thereby established; this is so just because it might not be clear that something he or she said was part of the prophetic message. Indeed it might be clear that it was *not* part of that message: for example, a messenger who seems credible might say so.

Now the questions I want to consider arise with respect to both of the issues I just distinguished: the issue of establishing messengership and the issue of establishing the message. To simplify matters, therefore, I just set aside the issue of establishing the messengership of the messenger, ignoring those parts of the passage quoted earlier in which Ibn Arabi appears to be talking about a proof that would establish this. Instead, I focus on Ibn Arabi's claim that "the *message* of the one who is sent must be established for the one to whom it is directed," and ask what this might amount to. We can leave it as an open question whether the message being established would, or might, involve the recipient of the message having it proved to him or her along the way that the messenger who has communicated that message is reliable, though Ibn Arabi does seem to have cases of that sort in mind.

To turn then to the crucial issue: what does it mean to say that *a clear and manifest proof of a message is established for someone*? I take the answer to this question to have a number of parts. For one thing, a case that makes it reasonable to believe and unreasonable not to believe must be made. It might be a manifestly sound argument, or a combination of such arguments, or really compelling evidence of one sort or another. Following Ibn Arabi, or, rather, his translator, I use the term "proof" as shorthand for all such ways in which it might be made reasonable to believe and unreasonable not to believe. It seems appropriate to focus on something along the lines of a proof, so understood. How could someone reasonably be blamed or criticized or found fault with in any respect for failing to believe something for which a robust case of this sort has not been made?[12]

Of course a proof could be difficult to understand. For example, comprehending it might require advanced study in logic. Someone who has not undertaken advanced study in logic could hardly be blamed for failing to grasp such a proof and hence for nonbelief that issues from that failure. So perhaps what would be relevant would instead be having been presented

---

[12] This thought may also be relevant to, and may provide reason to reject, one part of Ghazali's view on the situation of nonbelievers. Someone could learn about the claims made by a prominent religious figure or by a religious tradition but not be provided with a compelling reason to endorse those claims, in which case they could hardly be blamed for failing to do so. (They might still be at fault for *arrogantly or negligently* failing to endorse those claims. It's just that if they had not done so *arrogantly or negligently*, they could have done so reasonably.)

with a proof that is accessible to you, one that you have the ability to under-stand. Failure to believe subsequent to being presented with *that* sort of proof might be thought to render one ineligible for salvation.

However, a proof can be such that you have an ability to understand it, and yet you might *not* understand it. You might be busy or fail to think your way through it. So perhaps we should think of the relevant condition as a matter of being presented with a proof that is both understandable *and understood*. Failure to believe subsequent to being presented with a proof that satisfies *this* condition, or, rather, this combination of conditions, might be thought to render one ineligible for salvation.

Ibn Arabi may be adding yet another condition that, in his view, must be satisfied if nonbelief is to make one ineligible for salvation. He may also be saying that those who are at the receiving end of the proof *must actually be convinced by it* if nonbelief is to make them ineligible for salvation.[13] This may be part of what Ibn Arabi has in mind when he mentions various things (a message, "clear and manifest proofs") that must be "established" for the person "to whom it is directed." This reading is, I think, also suggested by his contrast between, on the one hand, clear and manifest proofs and, on the other hand, signs that have within them "*obscurity or equivocality such that some people do not perceive what [they prove]*" (my italics). The implication seems to be that what would render someone ineligible for salvation is being provided with a clear and manifest proof – one that is not obscure or equivocal – and perceiving what it proves, which is to say being convinced of its conclusion. (There is some similarity here with the case of the sixteenth-century Dominican Francisco de Vitoria, who insisted that no one "could be culpable for their rejection of the Gospel unless it had been presented to them in a convincing manner" [Madigan and Sarrió, 2016: 89].)

And it might not be enough *to have been convinced* by such a proof. For example, you might at one time judge an argument to be sound but later change your mind. Perhaps you no longer find the proof convincing. You may now question the reasoning you engaged in when you became convinced. Consequently, the relevant failure to believe would need to occur *while* one is convinced.

However, failure to believe under these circumstances would require con-siderable mental gymnastics and significant self-deception – if it is doable at all. It would involve actually being persuaded by a proof that such and such is the case while at the same time refusing to acknowledge that such and such is

---

[13] For a reading of Ibn Arabi along these lines, see Chittick (1994: 156). For another reading, see Khalil (2012: 60ff.).

so. This is a space so small that few, if any, could occupy it. Maybe there is no space at all here. This is so if what would be involved is believing while at the same time not believing. (What is under discussion here is very different from refusing to *act* in accordance with beliefs of which you are persuaded. For example, you might be persuaded that you should oppose publicly a war you believe to be unjust and yet you might fail to do so. Such situations occur all the time.)

After various clarificatory steps, what we have ended up with is the idea that only nonbelievers who (a) encounter a case that makes it reasonable to be convinced and unreasonable not to be convinced and who (b) are in fact convinced by this case, but who nevertheless refuse to hold the relevant belief even while being convinced, are to be understood as ineligible for salvation on account of their failure to believe. Correspondingly, nonbelievers who have not encountered such a case, or who have encountered it but do not understand it, or who have encountered and understood it but are not convinced by it, or who were convinced by it but are no longer convinced, are not to be excluded from salvation on account of their failure to believe.

Nonbelief under the conditions mentioned also seems less and less likely to occur as we go down the list of options in the order in which I have introduced them. And as we go down that list, fewer people are excluded and more are included. So what we have here are increasingly inclusivist accounts of the conditions that would exclude outsiders from salvation.

What we end up with after the series of clarifications outlined earlier is also a *generous* view; indeed, let's call it "the generous view." Ibn Arabi says that it "has within it a tremendous mercy" – assuming of course that the generous view, as I have just characterized it, is what he has in mind. (The fact that he describes his view as "[having] within it a tremendous mercy" is perhaps evidence that this *is* what he has in mind.) In any case, the generous view, irrespective of who endorses it, is attractive just because it is generous.

Incidentally, what is under discussion here – both in the case of the generous view and in the case of the various closely related views we encountered in this section while making our way to the generous view – probably is understood by anyone who advocates it as an excluding condition – a sufficient condition of being ineligible for salvation. In turn, the *absence* of this condition is taken to be a necessary condition of being eligible for salvation, and hence a necessary condition for achieving salvation. On the other hand, presumably the absence of the excluding condition in question is not taken to be a sufficient condition of achieving salvation. The thought is just that someone in whose case the excluding condition is absent, which is to say they are not ineligible for salvation because of their nonbelief or because of their nonbelief under particular circumstances, may be ineligible for salvation for some other reason. Perhaps not caring even a little bit about the justice, love, and peace that is central to the thinking of Madigan and Sarrió might have this consequence. Being totally indifferent to the interests of other forms of life that have interests, or torturing animals for entertainment, for example, might also be good candidates. (So what we are considering in these examples is the possibility that a *moral* requirement might also be necessary for salvation.) Hence even the generous view, along with its somewhat less generous cousins from which we distinguished it while clarifying it, is compatible with a pessimistic view of the salvation of outsiders, once all relevant factors are considered, though such pessimism is in no way suggested either by the generous view or by the alternatives discussed.

3.4 A Few Observations about Being Generous

According to the generous view, the condition (having to do with belief) that would make one ineligible for salvation would involve currently being persuaded by a proof that such and such is the case and yet not believing it to be so. However, if the human situation is religiously ambiguous, along the lines outlined in Section 1, a proof of any of the available religious alternatives is not to be had. Instead, a variety of positions on matters of religious significance may reasonably be endorsed. If this is so, a condition specified by the generous view would never obtain. And in that case, no one is ineligible for salvation on this account. And the same point applies to the various less generous views that we canvassed along the way and that also require proof if nonbelief is to make a person ineligible for salvation. Matters that are debatable and open to reasonable disagreement on the part of reasonable people – as is the case for matters of religious significance – just are not suitable for a belief requirement.

Some remarks from John Sanders introduce another area of inquiry. Sanders writes as follow: "[A] young woman with whom I spoke said she was not interested in Christianity. I later found out that she had been sexually abused by an elder in a church. Had she really been evangelized? What about Jews and Muslims who filter the gospel message through Auschwitz, Christian persecution, the crusades or Western imperialism?" (Sanders, 2016: 141). Obviously, what Sanders is asking here is, in part, the question of who has been evangelized or who has been reached with the Christian gospel message. However, his remarks also invite us to think more broadly about factors that might make religious belief difficult or even impossible for people so that they are not at fault for not believing.

Inculpable obstacles to belief certainly could and, I have no doubt, sometimes *do* include the consequences of sexual abuse. Such abuse might compromise a person's ability to trust relevant religious authorities or leaders or even his or her ability to trust in general. But other experiences (or discoveries or, in general, situations) might have the same consequences. A discovery that the authorities or leaders in question are wrong on many matters might also compromise a person's ability to trust those authorities. Another possibility is that the typical advocate of the views that you are being urged to endorse may be unimpressive – perhaps because of their gullibility or their bigotry or the narrowness of their loyalties or their failure to comply with what they declare to be their own ideals or for that matter their tendency to denigrate outsiders – leaving you feeling that you do not want to be associated with them. Or, to turn to another type of case that Sanders mentions, actions done by those who have acted in the name of the relevant religion or who have a close association with it may be so outrageous or cruel or unwise, for instance, that it is difficult even to hear what their coreligionists have to say. Many religions have associated with them embarrassing historical episodes of cruelty or violence or abuse of one sort or another.

Madigan and Sarrió write that, in the case of the Catholic Church, "it took several centuries for [members of the Church] to begin to acknowledge that their own moral failures could be the stumbling block that prevented others from recognizing Christ in the community of the baptized" (Madigan and Sarrió, 2016: 71, also 94–96). They mention again in this context the Dominican Francisco de Vitoria, who, "in the wake of the Spanish discovery of the New World . . . insisted that [the *Indios*] could not be considered culpable for having refused to accept the Christian message as it was declared to them by the Spanish colonizers: the scandalous behavior of the conquistadores, and, at times, of the preachers themselves, was a hindrance to the acceptance of the truth of the Christian message" (Madigan and Sarrió, 2016: 71). I have no doubt that equally candid members of all or most other religions could adduce their own embarrassing historical episodes.

So there are various ways in which information about, or experience of dealing with, religious authorities or leaders might make belief difficult. It might also make belief unreasonable. I am thinking of cases in which you have believed what people have said because they have seemed generally reliable: their testimony has been part of what has made your belief reasonable. A discovery, or even a suspicion, that they are not generally reliable might therefore sabotage the reasonableness of belief.

An obstacle to belief might take a different form. Someone might be convinced by some other view, or might have been brought up to believe that the view they are now encountering is false (Madigan and Sarrió, 2016: 89). Or they might come to the conclusion that the human religious situation is religiously ambiguous.

To sum it up, there are manifold ways in which people might become resistant to belief through no fault of their own. I have merely mentioned some examples. One implication of this array of possible obstacles for which a person may not reasonably be blamed is that we have little chance of ever knowing about another person's situation in this regard. To make a judgment in any particular case in which someone does not believe, and in particular to determine whether they are at fault for their failure to believe, you would have to know whether there were relevant obstacles and, if so, what role they played; this will generally be impossible to tell. It may even be impossible for the person himself or herself – the person who does not believe – to tell. (To revisit the sort of case from Sanders with which we began this discussion, a person might not recall the damaging sexual abuse, or he or she might recall it but might not understand its damaging consequences for his or her capacity to believe, should there be such consequences; the thought might never have occurred.) To assume that someone who does not believe the tenets of any particular religion is so situated because of some fault on his or her part lacks justification just as it lacks generosity.

What we have at hand is also a set of possible reasons why someone who is presented with a proof that he or she understands might not actually be convinced by it. Hence even if there were a proof, it might not convince someone through no fault of the person who is not convinced. And, according to the generous view – the view that has emerged as most plausible – nonbelief in cases in which someone has not been convinced would not render them ineligible for salvation.

A final point. There are many beliefs that recommend themselves to us in the strongest way and that we nevertheless find people unreasonably rejecting. And yet we often take, and should take, a relaxed approach to their doing so. Thus there are flat-earthers (see flatearthsociety.org) and people who deny that human beings have ever been on the moon in spite of the overwhelming evidence to the contrary in both cases. Probably the right thing to say in many such cases is along these lines: "it takes all types." Or "live and let live." Unreasonably ignoring the available evidence on such matters as the shape of the earth or whether people have been to the moon is unwise and idiosyncratic, and can be annoying, no doubt. But even the mildest penalty in such cases would be inappropriate.

What the generous view says is that what would exclude from salvation is refusing to believe while being convinced by a compelling case. If this sort of thing occurs at all, then those who pull it off are *very* unwise and *very* idiosyncratic. But why should being in such a state inevitably be salvifically disastrous? Why not adopt a "live and let live" and "it takes all types" approach in this case? *That* would be generous.

4 Religious Diversity and Religious Progress

> The adventurer set forth gallantly and with good cheer. He explored, he cast about, he went hither and he went thither. He paid careful attention to everything he encountered and to all he witnessed. He never felt that in order to keep himself afloat, others must sink. He never felt that for him to breathe, he might use up all of the available oxygen. For him to sing, others did not need to be silent. And he himself fell silent when he thought that silence was called for.
>
> (From *The Islander* by Adam Satu)

4.1 Introduction

What stage should we human beings consider ourselves to be at in our religious development? Are we in our infancy? Or our adolescence? Are we close to maturity or even fully mature, religiously speaking? Do the religions as we know them represent the completion of human religious development so that all of the major religious ideas and innovations there will ever be have already appeared? In that case, we have gone as far as we are capable of going, and hence as far as we are ever going to go, in this regard. Or, on the other hand, might we just be starting out in our religious evolution, so that currently available religious options, and all religious developments to date, are merely the first rude efforts of a species in its religious infancy?

The Canadian philosopher J. L. Schellenberg has recently made some thought-provoking observations about these matters. He proposes that we may be in the early stages of the development of intelligent life on earth and currently living through the infancy of our species. He observes that religion too may be in its infancy and we may be religiously immature (Schellenberg, 2007: chapter 3, and Schellenberg, 2013: chapters 1–4).

Schellenberg points out that if we do not destroy ourselves or suffer a massive catastrophe, human beings and our biological descendants may have as much as a billion years of life on earth ahead of us – a period that would dwarf the brief moment of human history that has already passed. And future humans or descendants of humans may develop mental powers that currently are unimaginable to us. Indeed, we can provide a simple inductive argument to the effect that future hominids will have brains that are larger, more complex, and more intelligent than ours.

I think that Schellenberg may well be on to something here. It is indeed possible that we are in our infancy, religiously speaking, and that our entire way of proceeding religiously is very primitive. While it could turn out that the religions of the distant future will closely resemble one or more of the religions of today, this seems questionable. Again a simple inductive argument is available: consider, say, any 10,000-year period in the past, and note the extraordinary religious changes that humanity has undergone in that period. If anything, it seems reasonable to expect the pace of religious change to increase, in line with, say, changes in science and in other rapidly changing aspects of the human situation and of course because of all of the future relevant changes, for good or ill, that will occur but that we are currently unable to anticipate. Forms of religion that we cannot now imagine may well emerge in the future. Indeed, it seems reasonable to expect this to occur. And the farther out into the future we extend our reflections in this regard, the more reasonable it is to suspend judgment about the forms that religion and, more broadly, human responses to matters of religious significance may take. And this is so whether human creativity is the major factor contributing to future religious evolution or whether instead future developments will be mainly the product of input from an external source such as a divine revealer, or for that matter a product of contributions from both of these sources.

Schellenberg has also made some interesting observations about factors that may have impeded our progress during our relatively short period of systematic religious reflection. These include the brevity of that reflection: it has been engaged in for just a few thousand years, and during that time we have had many other things to do. (Schellenberg, 2007: 70) Other potential obstacles arise from "moral, psychological, and social aspects of the human condition" (Schellenberg, 2007: 71). These include flaws such as our self-importance, greed, and dogmatism and the fact that we are prone to rivalry (Schellenberg, 2007: 72, 3). We lack patience and prematurely seek intellectual gratification. There is also the fact that people are attached to their world-picture, whether it involves religious belief or religious disbelief, and are difficult to budge once settled on a position (Schellenberg, 2007: 81). In addition, we are too focused on protecting our beliefs and on defeating the beliefs of others (Schellenberg, 2007: 74). Even virtues such as loyalty have been obstacles (Schellenberg, 2007: 76ff.). The same goes for emotions such as jealousy, envy, and anger, as well as positive emotions such as gratitude or love. We also suffer from what Schellenberg calls the "end of history illusion" (Schellenberg, forthcoming). People in the grip of this illusion, insofar as it exhibits itself with respect to matters of religious significance, think they have no further to go religiously, and indeed that there *is* no further to go religiously.

In these points too I think Schellenberg may be correct: these are all at least *potential* obstacles to religious progress. I would just add that the fact that religion has played so many functions in human life should also be mentioned in this context. For example, religion has had a *behavioral* function where this includes providing guidance in areas of life in which people need guidance. The religions have had a *therapeutic* role: for example, they help their adherents to cope with tragedy, hardship, distress, bereavement, disappointment, and with difficult situations of many sorts. The religions sometimes contribute to social stability. They also serve to *sacralize* important events such as birth, initiation into adulthood or into the religious group itself, and milestones in the life of a community, such as planting season or harvest. The fact that religions have played these and other important social and psychological functions in human life may have constituted, and may now constitute, an additional set of obstacles to religious progress. It may have made for conservatism and for excessive caution in reflection. There is always a lot at stake.

In light of where he takes us to be in our religious development, Schellenberg makes some proposals about preparing for the future. He advocates a new conception of inquiry in which we imagine ourselves as "members of a transgenerational community that may together solve the deepest intellectual problems baffling us today – or the even more interesting problems into which they may evolve" (Schellenberg, 2013: 36). He proposes that we make "a conscious and deliberate attempt to push transcendently interested religious thought and feeling further than it has yet gone" (Schellenberg, forthcoming). And he rightly highlights the value of attention to a diversity of religious perspectives in this undertaking. Thus he bemoans "how little attention, in our short tenure on the planet, has been given to open and wide-ranging exploration of alternative religious ideas – that is, to the exposure and discussion, from the perspective of a pure desire for understanding, of many alternative forms of transcendent and ultimistic ideas, both old and new" (Schellenberg, 2013: 145). These are challenging and even inspiring ideas.

4.2 Religious Progress

I propose that religious progress is best understood as combining two rather different elements. First, there is the matter of achieving a deeper understanding of the truth, of what is the case, of how things are. I refer to this as *progress in understanding*.[14]

Second, there is *practical progress*. For example, progress in the case of the behavioral function will be exhibited in, say, the extent to which participation

---

[14] In this and the next section I draw on McKim (2018) and McKim (forthcoming).

in a particular religious tradition leads people to be wiser, kinder, more sensitive, more generous, more concerned about justice, more inclined to care for the earth, more inclined to eschew avoidable violence, and the like. Correspondingly, progress in this area will make people more inclined to oppose cruelty, corruption, unfairness, ruthlessness, arrogance, the exploitation of others, bigotry, intolerance, indifference toward the outsider, abuse of the earth, abuses of power, and so on. And there is the question of whether a religion confers legitimacy on cruel or corrupt leaders and on ecologically destructive practices or, on the contrary, encourages people to challenge such leaders and such practices. And does what participants characterize as contact with, or absorption in, or worship of, or guidance by, or communication with, a putative religious ultimate have such consequences as those mentioned in the lives of those who report on such experiences? What is under discussion here is religion as it actually is, and not religion as it could be or as it should be or as its adherents wish it to be or for that matter imagine it to be. The question is whether a religion, as practiced, actually has the effects mentioned, and whether it has those effects now and not just that they are promised in some future dispensation.

Needless to say, practical progress of the various sorts mentioned often occurs in the complete absence of religion. Thus people can become wiser, kinder, more sensitive, more generous, more concerned about justice, more inclined to care for the earth, or more inclined to eschew avoidable violence, and the like, because they are persuaded to do so by secular factors – by, say, impressive civic organizations or by heroic individuals, with little or no role played by religion. Indeed this is a challenge that religions face: being relevant to the occurrence of such progress by making, and encouraging and promoting, practical progress.

The issue of whether people are influenced by their religious participation to care for the earth merits special emphasis. One reason this is so is that our survival and probably our flourishing as a species is a prerequisite for human religious progress. And our flourishing, and perhaps even our survival, requires that we avoid serious ecological disruption.

Broadly speaking, practical progress can be divided into progress with respect to how we deal with other human beings, including religious others, and progress with respect to how we deal with the world around us, including other animals, the landscapes we occupy, and so on. And there is another respect in which practical progress is best understood to have two dimensions. On one hand, there is the matter of *understanding* certain things: for example, an understanding of what others need and of what it is to be appropriately related to other species and to nature as a whole will an important resource when it comes to how we deal with others, with other species, and so on. (Because practical progress has this dimension, it partly consists in progress in understanding.) On the other hand, there is the matter of those resources being deployed or implemented. The latter issue has to do with how people live. Especially important is the matter of how large numbers of people live across generations.

4.3 Steps toward Religious Progress

How should we set about preparing to make religious progress, where this is understood to include both elements mentioned – both progress in understanding and practical progress? I propose a twelve-step program for this purpose. This, like the twelve-step program outlined in Section 1, has a number of interconnected components, to some of which I have already alluded. The purpose of *this* twelve-step program is to promote religious progress in all of its aspects, including with respect to how we see religious others.

1. The first and most obvious step is to make the topic of religious progress – its character, the very possibility of its occurrence, possible obstacles to it, how to prepare for it, the attitudes it might require, and so on – a widely discussed topic. Systematic reflection about how to circumvent whatever obstacles to religious progress there may have been, and there may be now, tackling these head-on, is central to taking this first step. Identifying and understanding such obstacles may take us a long way toward circumventing them. If the currently existing religions have labored to date while hampered by such obstacles, these religions may take off in unanticipated directions and surprise us with new insights if they are less constrained.

2. We need to think systematically about the sort of religious leadership that would help us to make religious progress. For one thing, existing religious leaders – clergy, elders, imams, priests, ministers, rabbis, and so on – might make the promotion of religious progress more of a priority. Another step is to ensure that future leaders will be sensitized to these issues, probably by integrating discussion of religious progress into their training. And we might need a cohort of leaders whose project would be to promote religious progress, who learn all they can about what it might consist in, who reflect on the institutions it would require, and whose job description includes helping with the implementation of this twelve-step process or, better, an improved version that emerges from future reflection.

3. Religions, as currently constituted, should see themselves as part of the broad, multifaceted, continually evolving history of the religious development

of humanity, a history that may have a long future and that may involve major developments that we cannot currently envisage – even if they also see themselves as a definitive part of that history and see their tradition as a major breakthrough.

4. We should all team up together and pool our efforts, with what have been religious foes, or at any rate groups that have operated independently of each other, becoming allies and fellow explorers in pursuit of religious progress. We should cultivate arrangements in which we are open to learning about others and they are open to learning about us. This requires everyone to learn as much as possible about the great variety of religions and their history and development. Systematic collaborative reflection about how to make progress might help us to unearth possibilities that no one has yet considered. Actually, if the human religious situation is ambiguous, as defined, there is no alternative to a collaborative approach.

5. Because of its importance, we should expect the religions to endorse the magnanimous outlook, as outlined in Section 1. This attitude will promote effective cooperation with others. Thus the promotion of this outlook should be incorporated into the training of future religious leaders, so that they have an understanding, however rudimentary, of the teachings, history, insights, experience, and so forth, of others. Likewise an effort should be made to incorporate this outlook into religious observances. Taking this step will require opening up more of the vast array of existing religious perspectives to humanity as a whole. It will involve becoming curious about what they have to say, about their distinctive insights, and about them. This is religion that has as part of its project grasping the religious views of others. It will also involve coming to see others as one's peers in various respects. Magnanimity and the search for truth are intimately related to each other; thus a willingness to learn from others, which is one component of magnanimity, will promote the search for truth.

6. We should think systematically about new institutions that might help us to make religious progress. What are needed are institutions that would permit the investigation of a lot of possibilities in the mode of magnanimity and that would help us to implement this twelve-step program or, again, an improved version of it. These institutions would encourage recognition of the legitimacy of various other religious practices and sensibilities. Some might be modified versions of already existing institutions or draw in one way or another on one or more currently existing religious traditions. The needed institutions would also attempt to take account of developments in many other areas, drawing in the

process on what can be contributed by social scientists, philosophers, experts on religion, people with relevant expertise in the sciences, and so on.

7. We should cultivate any insights that may have already been developed. Even a religion whose overall interpretation of how things are is largely mistaken may be an authentic response to something real and may have some unique insights. Since it is difficult to tell which traditions have made progress, or are about to do so, or are well situated to do so, this calls for everyone to adopt an exploratory and inquisitive approach to others and to how they understand things. For all we know, posterity may conclude that even by now *significant* progress has been made by one or more religious traditions. If some progress may have been made, everyone should be trying to see what green shoots that merit cultivation there may be, even in unexpected places. Indeed, it is odd to assume that entire religions that have flourished for millennia have nothing to teach outsiders. Consequently, a vast expanse of religious resources opens up before each of us. To get some remote grasp of, say, the religious experience of others is an immensely difficult task, not to mention everything else that is to be learned about others. It is best to be humble in the face of this immensity. It is easy to see how unsatisfactory it would be in other fields of inquiry – in, say, literary criticism, physics, economics, or philosophy – if there were disagreement on central issues and the various factions or schools of thought were nevertheless to ignore what they might learn from others.

Incidentally, it might be possible to get widespread cooperation in this venture since it treats many traditions as possible sources of progress. Each tradition can expect, and would be guaranteed, an audience from the others, becoming an object of reflection, and being seen as a possible source of insight. So each can enjoy the benefit of being taken seriously by others though this coin has another side, namely the need to extend the same courtesy to others, taking them and their religions seriously.

8. The study of religion, and of all scholarly work relevant to religion – including, say, relevant work in the academic study of religion such as comparative religion and in the social scientific study of religion, history, philosophy, textual scholarship, cosmology, biology, neuroscience, and anthropology – should be integrated into the practice of religion. For example, relevant work in such fields should be reflected in the understanding of the tradition and of its history and development that its members have. Relevant scholarship includes work that deals with matters such as the historical accuracy of claims associated with religious traditions, and it also includes work on what sort of beings we are and on how it came about that there is a universe – indeed all matters that the religions

purport to describe. It also includes work in the philosophy of religion and in theology that deals with, say, the coherence and plausibility of various ideas and proposals. Moreover, learning about the variety of religious perspectives and about their history and development requires taking account of what the relevant academic fields have to say: if we are to have an accurate and objective understanding of any insights that others may have achieved and of their perspective in general, relevant academic scholarship is essential. The plan is not to turn everyone into a scholar of these matters, but there can be broad recognition that the leadership should distinguish itself in this area and be familiar with the relevant fields and that ordinary folk should do the best they can in such respects, availing of all relevant opportunities. Each of us has to try to navigate our way across the great seas of relevant information that now confront everyone who reflects about matters of religious significance.

9. Religious traditions and communities can help in additional ways. They can encourage their members to take the aforementioned steps. Also, for various reasons, the pursuit of religious progress needs to be integrated with religious life. And such a life is unlikely to be a solo enterprise, normally needing for its maintenance a community of like-minded practitioners. Thus new ideas about how to approach things religiously will need expression in shared religious practice, sometimes on an experimental basis.

Lived religion is important for progress in many respects. There is the issue of what people intuitively feel to be the case after long-term experience dealing with the vicissitudes of life while looking at the world from a particular religious perspective and long-term careful contemplation. For example, does it feel to religious participants that their experience corroborates their outlook, or are they, on the contrary, left wondering why it fails to do so and hankering for something more satisfying? And only lived religion can reveal whether living in accordance with any particular religious perspective actually makes people wiser, more concerned about others, less willing to engage in or facilitate avoidable violence, more concerned about the future of life on earth, and so on. There is no other way to tell whether a religion actually amounts to what its adherents claim it to be.

10. Next, there are some experiments that can fruitfully be engaged in. Suppose you are, say, a Shiite Muslim and, for whatever reason, you immerse yourself in a new religious context. Perhaps you find yourself in a Catholic parish in the west of Ireland and you enter fully into the local Catholic community, attending mass and fully participating in the relevant religious practices, having your children make their first communion, and so on. Or perhaps you are a devout Hindu who encounters Wesleyan Methodism in this fashion. In each case, we have someone

from one tradition who enters another tradition and becomes a participant in it – in whatever rituals, observances, or festivals, for example, are distinctive of it and in general in its way of life. An outsider who participates in such a fashion in a host tradition would be in a position to have some access to the religious experiences that are characteristic of insiders, assuming there are such experiences, and in general to whatever reasons insiders may have for believing what they believe and for doing what they do.

To some extent we are here describing a process that someone can actually go through, and that some people probably have gone through. So there is nothing unrealistic about it. Individuals might fly solo in this regard, or it might be a group effort. A group effort would allow variations in personality, interests, motivation, intelligence, experience, knowledge, and more besides, to play themselves out in a variety of responses, so that the community can draw on the fruits of this variety. What we have here is a vast area for religious experimentation. This experimentation might even cast light on what people who are acquainted with more than one perspective *ought* to believe or on what it is reasonable to believe or on the range of appropriate options. Or it might be illuminating in some other way. We do not know what would emerge from such interactions.

11. We should also consider an idealized version of such experimentation – a related *thought experiment*. Here we imagine that the participants in question are *ideal* participants in the following respects. We assume that they have a great deal of relevant knowledge. So they have relevant training in comparative religion, in the social scientific study of religion, in philosophical and theological reflection, and in history. They are acquainted with relevant information in, say, cosmology, biology, and the neurosciences. They also know a great deal about the history and development of the relevant traditions and about relevant human religious experience. We also take them to be people of intellectual integrity. These participants challenge anything they find questionable and resist attempts to limit discussion and inquiry as they attempt to cope with all relevant information. Reflection about what would be believed by an ideal participant, so understood, might also provide guidance as to what one ought to believe, or about what it is reasonable to believe, concerning matters of religious significance, or, again, it might be illuminating in some other way.

12. Finally we should pursue interfaith initiatives in which different religions rally together to achieve practical goals. I have already mentioned the importance of jointly pursuing religious progress as such. Here my focus is on the possibility that joining together to solve important practical problems might be conducive to religious progress.

One impressive example of an organization designed to promote joint practical efforts is the Interfaith Youth Core (IFYC). The IFYC is active on many North American university campuses and aims to promote interfaith service projects engaged in by university students. The participants in these service projects are expected to take their collaborators as they are and to see what they can accomplish together, with everyone drawing on their own values, whether they are committed and devout members of a religious tradition who draw on the values of that tradition or, for that matter, they are relatively secular. So the IFYC approach is *conservative* in the sense that it proposes to leave everything as it is, religiously speaking, explicitly eschewing any attempt to influence or alter the religious perspectives that people bring to their shared service (see, e.g., Patel, 2007: 165). And yet I note that Eboo Patel, the founder of this organization, mentions in passing that a by-product of this sort of endeavor is "learning to see the faith of other people as just as deeply rooted and genuine as their own" (Patel, 2007:187). For some people, coming to see the faith of others to be as deeply rooted and especially as *genuine* as their own faith would actually be a significant shift in their perspective on religious others.

In any case, irrespective of the intentions or expectations of anyone who designs an organization or initiative of this sort, the reality is that if you work closely and effectively with others on practical service projects, you probably will think of the relevant others in a new way. For example, negative stereotypes and prejudices toward them are likely to fade. The thought that they are wicked or perverse or grossly defective in some way will be harder to sustain. It probably would make it easier to learn something from them. An enhanced awareness and understanding of them is likely to arise spontaneously from this sort of collaborative effort. This itself is religious progress.

The general area of inquiry here is how religious cooperation with a view to solving practical problems might make for religious progress – in addition to the progress, religious or other, that is involved in solving the practical problems in question. In his essay "Religious Diversity and Religious Environmentalism," Roger Gottlieb makes some creative observations in this area. He says that the religions are in fact becoming more open to each other and to the relevant sciences as they begin to understand the nature and extent of the environmental problems human beings are creating on the planet, and he mentions interesting examples from different parts of the world of interreligious cooperation with a view to solving such problems. He thinks that an ecological consciousness is developing across the traditions and that this suggests the possibility of a new shared religious outlook and fewer differences among the religious traditions. The need for this partly arises from the fact that traditional religious ideas are, he says, being found by those who espouse them not to be adequate for responding to the environmental crisis, so that many people are concluding that their own religion is not doing any better than the other religions in this regard (Gottlieb, 2011: 293). Each tradition is also inevitably dependent on the relevant sciences for an understanding of the character and scope of environmental problems (Gottlieb, 2011: 298). So the religions are led to turn outward in two respects. Gottlieb says too that "there is a sense among the vast majority of religious environmentalists that action on behalf of 'all of life' involves an expression of specifically religious values and has as its object the care of something that itself possesses at least a modicum of holiness. When we work together on this holy task . . . there is a sense in which we are all part of the same religion" (Gottlieb, 2011: 300).

The environmental scholar and activist Bill McKibben also proposes something along these lines. He says that a new religious understanding might emerge through interfaith environmental action (McKibben, 2001: 303). Collaborative action would "force those participating to think more seriously about what their traditions demand" so that diverse people of faith would "begin to knit together a new story of who we are and how we should act" (303) with "new and powerful visions emerging" (305). He mentions what happened to many churches in the United States when they supported the civil rights movement: "they searched more deeply through their traditions, and certain verses came to new and real life; certain themes emerged" (302). McKibben writes that "the deepest religious insights on the relation between God, nature, and humans may not emerge until religious people, acting on the terms indicated by their traditions, join [environmental] movements. The act of engagement will itself spur new thinking, new understanding" (302). He says that "[ecology] may rescue religion at least as much as the other way around" (305). Collaborative practical engagement might actually generate new religious insights. At the very least, it is worth trying. And, needless to say, environmental problems are an example – albeit a profoundly important example – of the practical problems to which this approach might be taken.

So we have a twelve-step program for the promotion of religious progress. Systematic collaborative reflection probably will yield additional possibilities. Would such steps as these actually yield religious progress? And, if so, how much? Frankly, it is impossible to tell. We do not know what would emerge from such an exploratory process; there is no way to predict its outcome. But once the possibility of religious progress is recognized, what alternative is there but to reflect about it as carefully and systematically as we can and to pursue it as best we can, even if we do not know what form it will, or might, take?

4.4 Concluding Reflections

Perhaps the religions would be more admired by their adherents if they were to pursue religious progress by taking steps such as these, including the promotion of the magnanimous outlook toward religious others, with all that this involves. Certainly outsiders would be more admiring. My own view is that religion that takes such steps is especially worthy of our interest, of being taken seriously and of our loyalty, and is itself making progress. It is responsive to the human situation.

However, various challenges and tensions are involved in taking such steps, and I want to probe some of these briefly. There is the challenge of recognizing the competing appeal of two sets of goods. On the one hand, there is the value of faithfulness to the home tradition, loyalty to it, identification with it, appeal to it by way of setting the standard for how one is to reflect and reason, and thinking of it as our source of insight as to what we should aim to be – even if all of this is tinctured with an awareness that what it is to be, say, faithful in this regard is not something fixed for all time, and that present and future realities may call for reinterpretation.

On the other hand, there is the importance of various ways of including others, of magnanimity, and of intellectual humility. There is what we know – or at any rate know we could know – about all that is involved in being a member of another faith. There is the need to create and maintain space, intellectually as well as socially and politically, for others to be as they wish to be and feel they should be. There is the need to acknowledge that others get on perfectly well without what we regard as the most worthy, richest, deepest, and most valuable things, the things for which we might readily make sacrifices and around which we organize our lives. This can be disquieting and disconcerting and even shocking to people of many religious perspectives, as can be the recognition that outsiders are often just as wise, just as honest, and so on, as we are, even when we are at our best. All of this has to do with facing up to the challenge that other traditions constitute for the home tradition, as well as with the intimately related issue of how one can best respond to that challenge.

There is, on the one hand, being pleased by the thought that other religions will flourish as they are and there is, on the other hand, wanting them to take steps that promote religious progress, even if doing so may change them considerably.

And to what extent is endorsement and, especially, implementation of the case I have made compatible with participation in the existing religions? For example, there is the question of how to go about combining whatever you learn from other traditions with the perspective you have in virtue of membership in your own tradition.

These waters, with the many currents that flow within them, are not easily navigated. And in the absence of institutions designed to facilitate progress, each of us must navigate these waters on our own. Each of us is, or at least can be, a pioneer and an explorer in this regard.

We could settle for saying that the religious traditions *will* modify themselves in light of the encounter with others, no matter what we think or say or do, so that all reflection about what form such change might take is idle. But surely it would be better if such changes were to occur subsequent to the sort of sustained reflection about the options that the steps outlined earlier require, and if such changes were to occur for good reasons.

As mentioned earlier, I think we should take a relaxed approach to the entire area of religious diversity. Let's see where human reflection about these matters goes over the next few millennia or so, and let's not assume we can currently say everything that needs to be said. In light of this last thought I advance my case in a somewhat exploratory way, as tentative moves that at least merit reflection, though it will not surprise the reader to learn that I also think that whatever direction future reflection about these matters may take, ideas along the lines of those I have outlined should have a place in it.

Bibliography

Aijaz, Imran. 2013. "Some Ruminations about Inculpable Non-Belief." *Religious Studies*, 49, 3, 399–419.

Aijaz, Imran. 2016. "The Islamic Problem of Religious Diversity," in Robert McKim (ed.), *Religious Perspectives on Religious Diversity*. Leiden: Brill, 162–175.

Alston, William P. 1991. *Perceiving God: The Epistemology of Religious Experience*. Ithaca, NY: Cornell University Press.

Anderson, Pamela Sue. 2011. "A Feminist Perspective," in Chad Meister (ed.), *The Oxford Handbook of Religious Diversity*. New York, NY: Oxford University Press, 405–420.

Basinger, David. 2002. *Religious Diversity: A Philosophical Assessment*. Burlington, VT: Ashgate.

Basinger, David. 2015. "Religious Diversity," in *Stanford Encyclopedia of Philosophy* (online) https://plato.stanford.edu/entries/religious-pluralism/.

Basinger, David. 2016. "The Role of Religious Diversity in Meaningful Religious Belief Assessment: One Professor's Experience," in Robert McKim (ed.), *Religious Perspectives on Religious Diversity*. Leiden: Brill, 209–228.

Chittick, William. 1994. *Imaginal Worlds: Ibn al-'Arabi and the Problem of Religious Diversity*. Albany, NY: State University of New York Press.

D'Costa, Gavin. 1990. "Christ, the Trinity, and Religious Plurality," in Gavin D'Costa (ed.), *Christian Uniqueness Reconsidered: The Myth of a Pluralistic Theology of Religion*. Maryknoll, NY: Orbis Books, 16–29.

DiNoia, Joseph A. 1992. *The Diversity of Religions: A Christian Perspective*. Washington, DC: Catholic University of America Press.

Eddy, Paul Rhodes. 2002. *John Hick's Pluralist Philosophy of World Religions*. Burlington, VT: Ashgate. (Reissued by Wipf and Stock in 2015.)

Eddy, Paul Rhodes. 2016. "Typology and Terrain: In Qualified Defense of the Standard Threefold Typology in Theology of Religions" in Robert McKim (ed.), *Religious Perspectives on Religious Diversity*. Leiden: Brill, 176–208.

Gellman, Jerome. 2016. "Jewish Chosenness and Religious Diversity: A Contemporary Approach," in Robert McKim (ed.), *Religious Perspectives on Religious Diversity*. Leiden: Brill, 21–36.

Gottlieb, Roger S. 2011. "Religious Diversity and Religious Environmentalism," in Chad Meister (ed.), *The Oxford Handbook of Religious Diversity*. New York, NY: Oxford University Press, 290–303.

Heim, S. Mark. 1997. *Salvations: Truth and Difference in Religion.* Maryknoll, NY: Orbis Books.

Hick, John. 1989. *An Interpretation of Religion.* New Haven, CT: Yale University Press.

Khalil, Mohammad Hassan. 2012. *Islam and the Fate of Non-Muslims: The Salvation Question.* New York, NY: Oxford University Press.

Khalil, Mohammad Hassan (ed.). 2013. *Between Heaven and Hell: Islam, Salvation and the Fate of Others.* New York, NY: Oxford University Press.

Khalil, Mohammad Hassan. 2016. "Islam and the Salvation of Others," in Robert McKim (ed.), *Religious Perspectives on Religious Diversity.* Leiden: Brill 149–161.

MacIntyre, Alasdair. 1988. *Whose Justice? Which Rationality?* Notre Dame, IN: University of Notre Dame Press.

Madigan, Daniel A. and Diego R. Sarrió Cucarella. 2016. "Thinking Outside the Box: Developments in Catholic Understandings of Salvation," in Robert McKim (ed.), *Religious Perspectives on Religious Diversity.* Leiden: Brill, 63–119.

McKibben, Bill. 2001. "Where Do We Go from Here?" *Daedalus: Journal of the American Academy of Arts and Sciences*, 130, 4, 301–306.

McKim, Robert. 2001. *Religious Ambiguity and Religious Diversity.* New York, NY: Oxford University Press.

McKim, Robert. 2012. *On Religious Diversity.* New York, NY: Oxford University Press.

McKim, Robert. 2016. "I'm Okay, You're Okay (More or Less)," in Robert McKim (ed.), *Religious Perspectives on Religious Diversity.* Leiden: Brill, 229–252.

McKim, Robert. 2018. "Why Pluralism Is Not Evil and Is In Some Respects Quite Good," in Jerome Gellman, Charles Taliaferro, and Chad Meister (eds.), *The History of Evil from the Mid-Twentieth Century 1950–2018 CE* (Volume VI of Chad Meister and Charles Taliaferro [eds.], *The History of Evil*). Abingdon: Routledge, 188–201.

McKim, Robert. Forthcoming. "On Making Religious Progress," in Paul Draper (ed.), *Current Controversies in Philosophy of Religion.* Abingdon: Routledge.

Mogahed, Dalia, Tom Pyszczynski, and Jessica Stern. 2011. "Religious Violence and Peace," in Chad Meister (ed.), *The Oxford Handbook of Religious Diversity.* New York, NY: Oxford University Press, 266–276.

O'Brien, Conor Cruise. 1972. *States of Ireland.* New York, NY: Pantheon Books.

Patel, Eboo. 2007. *Acts of Faith.* Boston, MA: Beacon Press.

Qadhi, Yasir. 2013. "The Path of Allah or the Paths of Allah? Revisiting Classical and Medieval Sunni Approaches to the Salvation of Others," in Mohammad Hassan Khalil (ed.), *Between Heaven and Hell: Islam, Salvation, and the Fate of Others*. New York, NY: Oxford University Press, 109–121.

Quinn, Philip L. 2000. "Towards Thinner Theologies: Hick and Alston on Religious Diversity," in Philip L. Quinn and Kevin Meeker (eds.), *The Philosophical Challenge of Religious Diversity*. New York, NY: Oxford University Press, 226–243.

Sanders, John. 2016. "Christian Approaches to the Salvation of Non-Christians," in Robert McKim (ed.), *Religious Perspectives on Religious Diversity*. Leiden: Brill, 120–148.

Schellenberg, J. L. 2007. *The Wisdom to Doubt*. Ithaca, NY: Cornell University Press.

Schellenberg, J. L. 2013. *Evolutionary Religion*. New York, NY: Oxford University Press.

Schellenberg, J. L. Forthcoming. "The Future of Religion: How Might Religion Make Progress?" in Paul Draper (ed.), *Current Controversies in Philosophy of Religion*. Abingdon: Routledge.

Taliaferro, Charles. 2011. "A Christian Perspective," in Chad Meister (ed.), *The Oxford Handbook of Religious Diversity*. New York, NY: Oxford University Press, 381–392.

Tuggy, Dale. 2015. "Theories of Religious Diversity," in *Internet Encyclopedia of Philosophy*. www.iep.utm.edu/reli-div/

Wainwright, William. 1988. *Philosophy of Religion*. Belmont, CA: Wadsworth.

Ward, Keith. 1990. "Truth and the Diversity of Religions." *Religious Studies*, 26, 1, 1–18.

Acknowledgements

Ben Miller, Bruce Rosenstock, and Kristin Seemuth-Whaley provided helpful and insightful comments on earlier versions of some of the contents of this Element. I am also grateful to Beau Ott and to an anonymous reviewer for Cambridge University Press for helpful and insightful comments on an earlier draft of the entire manuscript.

Permissions

Earlier versions of parts of Sections 1, 2, and 3 have appeared in my editor's introduction to Robert McKim (ed.), *Religious Perspectives on Religious Diversity* Leiden: Brill, 2016. An earlier version of some of the contents of Section 1.7 has appeared in my essay "I'm Okay, You're Okay (More or Less)," in *Religious Perspectives on Religious Diversity*. This material is used here, in modified form, with the permission of Brill, which I gratefully acknowledge. Earlier versions of parts of Section 4 are appearing in "On Making Religious Progress," forthcoming in Paul Draper (ed.), *Current Controversies in Philosophy of Religion*, Abingdon: Routledge. This material is used here, in modified form, with the permission of the editor, which I gratefully acknowledge.

Cambridge Elements ≡

Philosophy of Religion

Yujin Nagasawa

University of Birmingham

Yujin Nagasawa is Professor of Philosophy and Co-Director of the John Hick Centre for Philosophy of Religion at the University of Birmingham. He is currently President of the British Society for the Philosophy of Religion. He is a member of the Editorial Board of *Religious Studies*, the *International Journal for Philosophy of Religion* and *Philosophy Compass*.

About the series

This Cambridge Elements series provides concise and structured introductions to all the central topics in the philosophy of religion. It offers balanced, comprehensive coverage of multiple perspectives in the philosophy of religion. Contributors to the series are cutting-edge researchers who approach central issues in the philosophy of religion. Each provides a reliable resource for academic readers and develops new ideas and arguments from a unique viewpoint.

Cambridge Elements $\equiv$

Philosophy of Religion

Printed in the United States
By Bookmasters